Eddie Barlow

The Autobiography

EDITED BY EDWARD GRIFFITHS

Tafelberg

Tafelberg Publishers
a division of NB Publishers
40 Heerengracht, Cape Town, 8000
www.tafelberg.com
© 2006 The estate of E.J. Barlow

Eddie Barlow cover photograph and Hansie Cronjé picture
provided by Images24.co.za/Huisgenoot/YOU
Design by Susan Bloemhof
Set in 11 on 16 pt Janson Text
Printed and bound by Paarl Print, Oosterland Street, Paarl, South Africa
First edition, second impression 2006

ISBN 10: 0-624-04463-7
ISBN 13: 978-0-624-04463-5

Index

Introduction

 In August 2004, Eddie Barlow contacted me and told me that, with the help of his wife Cally, he had written the basis of a book relating the experiences of a bustling life. He asked if I would like to help with some editing and see the book published.

We met several times over the following 16 months, mulling over the project but never quite finding enough time to get the job done. It was, however, a job that needed to be done, because he had an extraordinary tale to tell… of cricket, of course, as a player and a coach, but also of farming and politics, of his beloved South Africa, and lastly, of facing up to the debilitating effects of a major stroke.

On 30 December, 2005, I received a telephone call to say Eddie had died in Jersey. I spoke to Cally a few days later and she said: "We must finish the book now."

I agreed.

Thankfully, Etienne Bloemhof shared our belief that this was the story of a great South African life that needed to be written, not just as a tribute to Eddie, not just to reflect the achievements of so many people with whom he worked and played, but also to inspire those who never met this effervescent, determined character and, through this book, will come to know what he represented.

It has been a privilege to be involved in its preparation.

Edward Griffiths
Halden Farm
August 2006

Chapter One – Thinking Big

If there is one central theme, in which I have always believed, it is this: the secret of life is to be positive, to try your best, to get on the front foot, get stuck in and give it everything.

That's what I have tried to do, in cricket and in every other aspect of my life. For many years, this approach seemed something instinctive inside of me. It was an attitude that just happened, and I struggled to explain exactly what I meant.

Then, not long ago, my wife Cally was rummaging through some papers that belonged to her late father, when she came across an anonymous poem entitled 'Think Big'.

I read the verses, and was taken aback. This was precisely what I believed, what I had always believed. My reaction was to ask Cally to make photocopies of the poem, so I could distribute a copy to each of the young cricketers I was coaching at the time in North Wales. This was what I wanted them to hear.

If you think you are beaten, then you are;
If you think you dare not, you don't;
If you'd like to win, but you think you can't
It's almost a cinch you won't;
If you think you'll lose, you've lost;
For out in the world, you'll find
Success begins with a fellow's will –
It's all in the state of mind

Full many a race is lost
Ere ever a step is run
And many a coward fails
Ere ever his work's begun;
Think big and your deeds will grow;

Think small, and you'll fall behind;
Think that you can, and you will –
It's all in the state of mind

If you think you are outclassed, you are;
You've got to think high to rise,
You've got to be sure of yourself before
You can ever win a prize
Life's battles don't always go
To the stronger or faster man,
But sooner or later the man who wins
Is the fellow who thinks he can.

This has always been so true for me… the man who wins is, indeed, the fellow who thinks he can.

As a schoolboy who loved all sports, as a developing cricketer who was fortunate to play the game all over the world, in England and Australia, as a South African who felt so proud to represent his country, and who, I hope, played a small part in building a country of which we can all be proud, as a father and husband, and as a coach – I have always tried to think big.

That's all you can do. Sometimes it worked out, sometimes it didn't, but it was never for a lack of effort.

Chapter Two – Early Days

I popped out on August 12th, 1940 and joined Mum, Dad and Norman. I don't know whether he wanted a brother but I am sure I was more than Norman had bargained for. He was five years older than I was, so it took a while before I could give as good as I got but then I certainly made up for lost time.

My father's family originally came from Manchester, in England, and it was my grandfather who took the decision to head south and build a new life at the foot of Africa. He eventually arrived in Mossel Bay where he started his business as a plumber.

By all accounts he was quite a character and it seems as if he might have got around a bit. During a visit to Mossel Bay, on the south coast of South Africa, in the late 1970s, I was accosted by a very attractive coloured girl, who announced that her name was Barlow and that she was related to me. She knew me as a cricketer, but thought perhaps I wouldn't want to speak to her. On the contrary, I was delighted to meet her, even though I thought she would have done better to be related to the wealthy Barlows of Rustenburg, rather than the Barlows of Pretoria.

In those days, large families were the norm. My mother, Dorothy, had three brothers, Frank, Kenneth and Bruce Winterton, and my father, John, was one of eight children. They were a very clever family and could turn their hands to almost anything.

Two days after Dad's youngest brother, Dave, was born, my grandmother died. Grandpa hired a nanny to look after all the children and shortly afterwards married her.

The uncles on my mother's side of the family were the bane of her life. They were all car-mad and spent most weekends stripping the car to see if they could make it go any faster. The trouble was they pursued this hobby in our driveway and were forever bringing smelly oily rags and dirty boots into the house. There was an old black Vauxhall of which they were particularly proud and it always seemed to be in pieces. When it was back together they would all pile in and declare it better than ever even if they had only managed to generate a tiny bit more speed.

My father, John, known to the family as Pops, was a lovely man but a total dreamer. His ship was always coming in and his ideas for making money were never-ending. He must have driven my mother mad when each pay day he would take his wages to the race track where his latest hot tip would crawl in last and she would be left to make ends meet with what was left.

Part of me envied him. How many of us are not dreamers, waiting for our ships to come in, all of them the treasure ships we read about as youngsters? Maybe I do Pops an injustice.

His love of cricket, rugby and soccer surpassed mine. He would often come home after watching Pretoria Boys High School (PBHS) play a match against King Edward's School (KES) and say, 'Hey kid, I liked the look of their fly-half,' or 'That number 6 batsman will go far'. He was always so enthusiastic and positive. If anybody says I owe a lot to my father, they are right.

Money was tight, but ours was a happy home, and Norman and I were never short of love and encouragement from both our parents. My mother was always called 'Girl' by my father, and she forever seemed to have several jobs on the go to try to make ends meet. She was also an expert on finding bargains at the sales. Underpants on special were not to be missed and twelve pairs would suddenly appear in the drawers.

'They were a bargain,' Mum would say.

We always seemed to be moving house, usually because a job would fall through and that meant we would have to be on the move again. Pops once got a job as a handyman at the SPCA, and Mum was taken on as a clerk. She decided to breed seal-point Siamese cats, and Dad did his bit by constructing a run outside my bedroom window. An animal shelter is rarely a quiet place, and this makeshift cats' home was no exception. Night after night, just when everything seemed to be settling down, some dog would start barking and then our cats would start yowling. It was bedlam, and sleep was nearly impossible.

Mum became quite a successful breeder in the beginning but then the neighbourhood toms got amongst the pure seal-points and there was hell to pay. Mum rushed around breathing fire and brimstone and threatened to sue everyone in sight for the damage done to her precious cats.

This constant uprooting and moving around made me determined that one day I would have my own house. With four of us in the family, space always seemed to be at a premium. In one flat we lived in, I slept on the balcony. That was fine in summer but the winters were a little chilly to say the least.

Of course, Norman and I played sport whenever we could, either just by ourselves, or with our mates.

At one point, when we were in Pretoria, we lived opposite a youngster called 'Tiger' Lance, who would grow up to become a great friend and teammate over the years. Back then, he attended Christian Brothers College, and we often found ourselves on opposing sides in school matches.

Tiger was a great source of stories, and I will never forget how we laughed when he told us about the time he was left to babysit his young twin brothers. Like most of us, Tiger had his fair share of small cups, won for various sports races, and he told the two small boys that he was in charge of the trials for the Olympic Games.

"Tonight is the Marathon trials," he declared, "and whoever wins will get the cup."

He had them running around the house lap after lap, with his sole intention being to tire them out. His plan worked and, as soon as he got them to bed, the two boys fell fast asleep in world record time.

My first formal education was at Waterkloof House Prep School, usually referred to as WHPS, pronounced 'Whips'. It was a happy place and, not long ago, I was browsing through a history of the school written by Mr Bob Hamilton, the former President of the Chamber of Commerce, Assocom. He was kind enough to write that 'Eddie Barlow was mentioned more times, and in more annual year books, than any other boy from his time or since'.

I'm not sure whether that is the case or not, but Mr Hamilton's history goes on to report:

The annual reports recorded that Eddie played for the first teams in cricket and soccer for four consecutive years, which was a rare and unique achievement. Although he was very young when first chosen, and hence much smaller than the other boys in the team and opponents, his determination and ability not only compensated any shortfall in size but also made him a player to be reckoned with from a young age.

As I read all this to myself, I had the sense that I was reading about somebody else. All I can remember is loving every match, and trying to appreciate every opportunity that came my way. For me, school was one long sporting festival, and I tended to look pretty scruffy at the end of the school day.

In fact, on one occasion, Norman was called to the headmaster to tell my mother to send a change of clothing because I could not leave the school to go home looking so dirty. I played sport every day so of course I was going to get filthy.

At one point, we played a match against Pridwin Prep School, from Johannesburg, and one of my opponents that day was a young man called Ray White, who would grow up to be fine cricketer and a distinguished administrator in SA Cricket.

I'll let Raymond tell the story:

It was the day when the two of us, Eddie and I, played in our prep school First XIs for the very first time. By the time I was ten years old, I had developed the dubious skill of flighting high looping leg breaks. It was not an art that I was able to extend into anything profitable beyond my early years, but by the time I had reached the Pridwin First XI, I had begun to harvest a considerable amount of wickets in schoolboy cricket.

Pridwin was a toffish kind of school, and my first match for them was against WPHS, a slightly less toffish school in Pretoria. Our team was captained by Toby Wade, the son of HF Wade, who had been the South African cricket captain in the 1930s. The young Wade gave me the ball when WPHS has lost four wickets and in no time I picked up another three by way of a couple of stumpings and a dodgy LBW decision.

The next batsman was a small boy with snow white hair and a ferocious glint in his eye.

My first ball to him was another cunning flighted spinner to which he jumped miles down the pitch and smashed it like a rocket straight past my head to the boundary. The following ball suffered the same indignity. Shaken by this on-slaught, I dropped the next ball too short and watched it disappear into the school buildings.

'Time to take your cap, Pinkie,' the tiny batsman scornfully shouted down the wicket in reference to the dirty pink caps that Pridwin players wore, and my woeful effort at troubling him. It was the first sledging I had ever encountered, and my first introduction to Eddie Barlow.

On the way home, Herby Wade told us, 'that boy will grow up to play for South Africa', and nobody disbelieved him.

It sounds like I was a cocky little guy in those days, and some people would say I never really changed.

From WHPS, I moved on to undertake my secondary education at Pretoria Boys High School, and a more impressive place would be hard to find. The setting was magnificent, with the main school building standing on a hill opposite the famous Union Buildings. The school was designed, like so many of the city's more important edifices, by Sir Herbert Baker. I always thought it looked rather like St Paul's Cathedral in London but, as callow schoolboys, I'm sure we did not appreciate its finer points.

A ring-bound book called 'Forty Years On' was produced, giving an account of my matriculation year, the class of 1957. I was lucky that my entry was written by Peter Eedes, my old mate.

He wrote to me the other day and called me 'Cussy'. The word made me smile because, so far as we were concerned, this was a term of endearment coined by another mate, Neil Morrison, in a rugby game. Apparently it was the 'in' name used by the local boys, who wore their hair in the latest style of the Ducktail. I must confess that I cannot for the life of me remember having a 'duck's arse', but then it was a long time ago.

Pete Eedes and I went through school together and then on to university. We were both mad keen sportsmen, but Pete excelled in the scholastic department. He became an excellent teacher but like many, found it hard to come to terms with what have become accepted as the new methods of teaching.

In my view, these so-called improvements are the reason for what seems to be a basic lack of discipline in many schools these days. I know it's not the politically correct thing to say, but we were all caned when we were schoolboys and I'm sure it had no negative lasting effect on us. On the contrary, it served to set down the line between right and wrong. Those cuts hurt like hell, but it was soon over and done with, and the cold water from the washroom basins quickly cooled down our throbbing posteriors.

My favourite subjects at school were Geography and English Literature, preferences that probably had something to do with the fact that both the teachers were rugby coaches.

Charlie Mulvenna taught Geography and on occasion was responsible for much mirth in the class. "Texas changed dramatically when they found oil there," he announced one day and from the back of the class came the voice of a redheaded Scot called Chris Angus. "Well, well, well." There followed the instant collapse of pupils and teacher together.

Pete Moerdyk taught English Lit. In my matric year, our prescribed works were *Hamlet* and Jane Austen's *Pride and Prejudice*. It took a long time for the numbskull rugby players like me to come to terms with what Jane had to offer, but I will always remember how Mr Moerdyk managed to bring *Hamlet* to life.

Will 'Snake' Hofmeyr was my Maths teacher and also the cricket coach. Maths was never my favourite subject, but his teaching made it bearable. He had gone to Oxford University and he hailed from the respected family of Hofmeyrs who have made a meaningful contribution to South Africa, politically and otherwise, over the years. His younger brother, Murray Hofmeyr was a brilliant sportsman, a cricketer and a flyhalf.

Will Hofmeyr would have died for a game of cricket and he couldn't do enough for us cricketers as a coach. We exploited his enthusiasm, and managed on many occasions to sidetrack a Maths lesson by lobbing in a few high balls and changing the subject to cricket.

There was one interesting moment with Snake at the nets. He loved his tea and, at around about half past three, the tea boy would arrive with a tray on which reposed his cup of tea with a small bowl of sugar beside it. I don't remember who it was, but one of the boys had mischievously poured half a bottle of Eno's Fruit Salts into the sugar bowl.

Snake sat down to enjoy his tea, having had a hard afternoon out on the field. I was batting at the time and all I heard from the boundary was him demanding to know: 'Which prune did this'. There was his lovely afternoon cup of tea frothing over with the Eno's he had unknowingly spooned into the cup.

He was the first coach I had come across who taught what today has become standard practice. He was very concerned about line and length and how important it was to stop throwing runs away, and he always made a point of setting field placings to stop the runs flowing freely. Nobody else was thinking along these lines in those days. Snake was truly ahead of his time.

He would sometimes regale us with stories of playing cricket at Oxford and Cambridge, which to us seemed a totally unattainable world. We had heard about these famous universities and seen pictures of them, but to be in the company of someone who had actually been there was something else.

When I eventually reached England, one of the highlights was playing against Oxford University on their ground. I remember feeling that, through Will's stories, I had somehow been there before.

One compulsory activity at PBHS was the Army Cadet Force. It didn't appeal to me at all, but every member of the school had to join up in Standard Six and stay there until Matric. We had to wear those awful itchy shirts and trousers that were agony in the heat and we drilled with out of date, army issue 303s.

The saving grace was that we were made to march to the tune of either a school bugle band or the school military band. The sound of the music was the only thing that kept me going. I longed to be a member of the band, particularly the one who banged the big bass drum. He was decked out in a leopard skin and everybody seemed to think he was the bee's knees.

One day Mr Abernethy, the headmaster, read out a notice asking if any boys wanted to join the bands.

'Report at first break to the music master, Mr Jandrell, in the Hall,' bellowed the Head. I couldn't believe my ears, and recognised this as my big chance. I had shown very little musical talent up till then. In fact, I think I may have been tone deaf, but I had inveigled my way into the choir, singing on Saturday mornings for the princely sum of 2s.6d, a much-needed boost to my funds, and also into the chorus of various school musical productions, and even secured the part of a policeman in *The Pirates of Penzance* by Gilbert and Sullivan. The chorus sang, 'A policeman's lot is not a happy one', and then I would add, 'Appy one'.

However, I was obsessed with the idea of being a member of the school band, so I decided to try.

"Barlow, what on earth are you doing here?"

"I want to join the military band, sir".

Mr Jandrell looked very sceptical but told me to go and get an instrument, which was lying under the stage. Crawling amongst the dust and spiders' webs, my eyes lit upon a large brass instrument, which I grabbed and dragged out. The teacher told me it was a double B flat Bombardon, which was something akin to a tuba. By the end of the day, I had learned to play three notes that I assumed would somehow blend in with the double bass drum.

After band practice I was told to take my instrument home and clean it. After finding some wire and rope, I tied the instrument to the front of my trusty bicycle and took it home, and put it in the corner of the sitting room, where it would be safe.

When Pops came home from work, he asked: "What is that bloody thing?" I informed him of my new interest, and was about to start polishing my new pride and joy. His only comment was 'Take it back, we can't afford the Brasso'.

That was the end of my musical career. There would be no Covent Garden, Royal Albert Hall or Madison Square Garden for me.

Rugby was my number one sport at PBHS. It seemed to come more easily to me than cricket at this stage of my life, and I played as a centre three-quarter, enjoyed it and seemed to climb the ladder of school teams rather quickly.

My first tour with the First XV was a trip to Grahamstown, in the Eastern Cape. The manager was George Batty, a popular history teacher who used to tell us all about the frontier wars. I enjoyed these tours, not just for competitive schools rugby but also because it gave me my first chance to see some of the country. We played St Andrew's, St Aidan's and Kingswood College, and were delighted to win all three matches.

Grahamstown was so cold that the water system froze up, so we emulated the British aristocracy and took cold showers. That was purgatory, but, when the hot water started to bubble through, it felt wonderful.

I remember it was on this tour that we met Eric Brotherton, a wonderful schoolboy sportsman. He was brilliant at all sports, but never became an international, most probably because he was too busy playing every sport that came his way.

Lasting friendships were formed on these tours, and I think it is important that schools should continue to tour the country, even if inflation means they would have to pay more than we did. I kept a scrapbook from that rugby tour to Grahamstown, and the costs of the tour were as follows: train fare per boy – £2.10s.6d; bedding (both ways) – 10s; meals (both ways) £1.3s; Total – £4.10s.10d. For lifelong memories, that was a bargain.

Another memorable experience was our tour to White River. Travelling by train, we left in the evening and arrived early the next morning, to be met by the parents of local schoolboys who loaded us into the back of their *bakkies* (small trucks) and took us off to the Kruger National Park. Breakfast was boerewors, grilled over an open fire and served with bowls of lovely fresh sweet tomatoes. We had been travelling overnight and had had no dinner so we certainly showed those Lowveld boys what eating was.

We then spent a wonderful day in the Kruger Park seeing most of the animals for which this reserve is so famous around the world. The farmers and their sons beat us hands down at spotting the game as we drove through the bush. Having been brought up in this special place, their eyesight was incredible.

The braaivleis is the South African equivalent of the barbeque and any excuse is given to bring out the braai. Every evening of the tour, one of the fathers would host a braai and we were expected to eat. Boy, that boerewors and tomato was good. It became probably my favourite meal. What could ever be better than sitting around an open fire on a warm evening with your dinner cooking right in front of you? Anybody visiting South Africa should try to spend time in the Lowveld, where boerewors is a speciality. Every butcher in every small country town believes his boerewors is the best.

We had been promised an opportunity to go hunting. Being so close to the Kruger Park, plenty of game tended to come across into the farms. Personally, I have never been a great hunter of buck and so forth, so I gave that a miss, but I was still impressed by some of my school friends' shooting skills.

They were incredibly accurate and it wasn't long before they had shot more than enough buck to make biltong to last a lifetime, or so we thought. Get fifteen to twenty rugby players sitting on a train with nothing to do and a sack of biltong soon disappears. I put biltong and boerewors at the top of my food list.

Even after all this hospitality, we managed to perform well in our match against White River High School, and we played fast, running rugby and ran out comfortable winners.

The farms in this eastern part of South Africa are incredible places, offering a fantastic quality of life, and many of the farmers had made money by creating eucalyptus plantations so they could supply the small wooden poles which, at that time, were widely used as supports in the mines. These farms were little gold mines in their own right, at least until an engineer developed a mechanical system which proved far more efficient, cheaper option. The wood was no longer required, and these farms suffered.

One of the features of eucalyptus is that it burns very well and, during our visit to White River, I got caught up in a team that was sent off to fight a fire in one of these plantations. If there was ever a time in my life when I have felt completely and utterly helpless, this was it.

Huge trees and dense undergrowth kept bursting into flames around us. How could we put it out? I didn't know. We were all relieved when we saw the *bakkie* coming over the hill, three or four miles away, and the people came to collect us. We were not far from being swept up in those huge flames.

It was an incredible experience, and I was left admiring the people who fight these fires, burning back and creating firebreaks. The noise of a veld fire in full fury is as terrifying as the heat from the flames that seem to envelop you. The sound of trees and bushes erupting into flame is like an explosion.

However, we survived our tour to the Lowveld, and headed back to Pretoria with a few stories to tell.

Touring was fun, but our greatest adversary on the rugby field was Afrikaans Seuns Hoërskool, known as 'Affies'. They were the school we wanted to beat the most and, in one match against Affies, a few days before my 16th birthday, I was tackled heavily and suffered severe concussion.

It felt as if I was becoming a marked man, especially when we played East Rand mining teams. I would hear someone shout 'Kry daai witkopsenter' ('Get the blond centre'), and, sure enough, not long afterwards I would be heavily tackled – that is, of course, if they could catch me. It was a good contest.

In my time at Boys High, there were six houses, three for dayboys and three boarding houses. The day houses were named after areas of Pretoria and my house was Town. Inter-house rugby matches were another source of potential aggro, and the boarders were always keen to beat the day 'bugs'.

Schools rugby was a physical game in those days. Everybody knew that, and my family better than most. My brother Norman had also played rugby for PBHS and I remember seeing him play for the school against Brits High School. He left their winger standing with a great break, but the Brits player turned, chased back and flattened my *boet* with a neck-high tackle. It would have been called a foul today, but it was regarded as OK in those days.

Pops was furious: I remember him talking of nothing else the whole way home. "If someone does that to you, you must have a reply to show who is in charge," he fumed. He said the three of us would have a training session the next day, and Pops was going to show Norman and me precisely how it was done.

We set off in a cavalcade of bicycles with Pops in the lead, talking incessantly about the morning's programme. He was going to be the tackler, I would be the centre and Norman would have to be the wing outside me.

Everything was set up, and Pops came in to tackle Norman, who handed him off. It was a beauty, catching Pops just below the temple. Down he went and he didn't move. "You've killed him," I said, in horror, whereupon a defiant voice emerged from the heap on the grass and saying: "I'm OK, lets keep going".

When we arrived home, Mum immediately saw something was wrong, and she did not hold back.

"John, you're not a boy anymore," she told him.

The hackles came up.

"Oh no? Well, we'll need a stretcher next time for him," Pops replied, jabbing his finger in Norman's direction.

Wars start easily. Everyone learned a lot that day, especially Mum, who kept out of future arguments.

As the winter drew to a close and rugby finished, the advent of summer led us to the cricket nets. Our school season lasted from September to the end of January the following year, and the highlights were usually the away matches against schools in Johannesburg. We travelled by train, which was always good fun with everyone together, lots of singsongs and laughter and the game of cricket to be played at the end of the journey. Many great games were played; some were won, others lost but we were always ready to be 'up and at 'em'.

I enjoyed my cricket days at Boys High, although there was one hiccup when I was relieved of the first XI captaincy because our teacher thought

I was making the players work too hard. I just felt we should do whatever we could to play as well as possible, and it seemed to me, even then, that fitness was important. Anyway, it wasn't a big deal. I still loved playing the game.

One of the highlights of the PBHS cricket season was a match between the first XI and a side organised by the Governor General, who afterwards hosted a reception at Government House. This mansion felt like a palace to us, as schoolboys, but the *piece de resistance* as far as we were concerned was the swimming pool.

We were not allowed to swim on these occasions, but a group of us thought we should maybe make a plan for another time. We used to go swimming, regularly and illegally at the Teacher Training College pool, where we tied our clothes to our bicycles so we could make a quick escape if we were discovered.

One night, maybe a week after the Governor General's match, six or seven of us cycled over to Government House, with no idea what kind of security we would find. We made our way to the side of the house where the pool was located and, as usual, we stripped off and tied our clothes to the bikes.

We climbed over the wall and had just dived into the fantastic cool water when, from nowhere, a couple of security men appeared. With much squealing, we legged it out of the pool, back over the wall and onto our bikes.

So there we were, riding as though the devil himself was chasing us, straight down Church Street through the middle of Pretoria, naked as the day we were born.

There was one other option for a refreshing dip on a hot summer's day, and that was the pool at the Pretoria Girls High School, but it was normally very heavily guarded by the formidable Mrs Nelson, the headmistress, and her staff.

The PBHS cricket season concluded with trials for the Nuffield Week, an annual festival started when Lord Nuffield, an Englishman, left a bequest to South Africa to help benefit sportsmen. The cricket authorities decided to create the Nuffield Weeks when, every January, each province fielded a team of their best high-school players to fight it out against each other.

The festival was hosted in a different town each year. At the end of the week the South African Schools side was chosen, and it was assumed that these young cricketers would form the future of South African Test cricket. To be selected in an SA Schools side was the overriding goal of every young boy.

I was selected to play at the Nuffield Week in 1956, but didn't do well and didn't feature in the Schools side. Things went better in the second and third year, when I played better and was chosen on both occasions for the South African Schools XI. No fewer than six of my teammates in that side went on to represent their provincial sides, some of them at a very young age.

The system worked well, and South African cricket benefited from providing such a good start for their young players and helping them on the tough road of international sport.

Our era yielded its fair share of great players. The star of my first year in the SA Schools team was a fast bowler from Boys High named Jackie Botten. His secret weapon was his slower ball, which he concealed brilliantly. It had batsmen groping all over the place and, on many occasions, being bowled. People talk about the slow ball today, but it is nothing new and Jackie Botten was a master.

Other exceptional schoolboy cricketers in my time were my old friends 'Tiger' Lance and Dennis Lindsay, the wicketkeeper. Dennis was involved in a rather unfortunate incident when he shaped to throw the ball back to the bowler. The batsman casually walked out of his crease, whereupon Dennis, who had not actually let go of the ball, promptly stumped him.

The umpires thought this was 'not cricket', and poor Dennis was given a roasting second to none. I remember he was distraught for days afterwards, but thank heavens these things occurred when we were young and resilient.

This was another way the South African system worked, because it gathered youngsters together, got the mischief out of them at an early age and taught them the difference between right and wrong early on.

Another lad who featured very strongly at that time was the great fielder, Colin Bland. If anything, he seemed to be an even more brilliant fielder when he played for the SA Schools side than he ever was as a Test player. Maybe he felt under less pressure in those days, and relaxed, and just got on with it.

Chapter Three – Rugby Days

After leaving Boys High, my enthusiasm for sport was such that I wanted to play cricket and rugby at the highest possible level. There was no question of playing one or the other. I enjoyed both.

At that time, in the late 1950s, the South African government offered a bursary to prospective teachers who signed up to study at the University of the Witwatersrand. Teaching was something I thought I would enjoy, so I decided that would be the best way to secure a place at this famous seat of learning. In my mind, I was going to become a geography teacher, mostly because that had always been my favourite subject.

First, I had to attend a Teachers College in Johannesburg to decide on the courses I was going to take at University. I was based at the Nockando residence with approximately 30 other students, all male. The female residence was not to far away, at the top of Melle St and needless to say, we were frequent visitors.

On one occasion, I had been playing cricket somewhere on the East Rand and Dennis Lindsay's dad had given me a lift back to the 'res'. Cricket had been demanding so much time that I had decided, that very day, to hang up my cricket boots and concentrate on my studies.

So I got back to my room, threw my cricket bag under the bed and left it there. The following Sunday morning we were in the sitting room of the residence when a chap came running in, asking if there was anyone who could play cricket. My ears pricked up immediately.

"We're nine down and playing on the Postage Stamp in the University grounds," he explained.

"I can play," I replied.

"Can you come right now?"

"Sure."

My brief period of retirement had ended, and I grabbed my bag from under the bed and raced off with him.

The Wits team were in serious trouble when we arrived. I was asked to bat at No.11 and, feeling in very good nick, proceeded to do the only thing I knew best, which was to hit the ball as hard as possible, whenever possible. My score mounted, past 100, and so did my partner's. It was quite a jolly affair. The runs enabled us to win the game and everyone was excited.

The captain asked afterwards: "Will you play cricket for Wits?"

"No, thanks," I replied.

"You must," he said. "See you at nets on Tuesday."

That was that. I had no choice, and I became the regular opening batsman for the University, playing in the Johannesburg First League, then known as the Premier League. However hard I tried to subdue my enthusiasm, sport took priority over learning and I soon immersed myself in cricket and rugby.

The cricket went well. I played for a strong Wits First XI and we won the Premier League for the first time. Our last match of the season, at Jeppe, ended in a tie and I managed a modest half-century. Two of my teammates, opening bowler Graham Bunyard and leg-spinner Sid Stanley, were unlucky not to be chosen for the South African team that toured England in 1960.

I was also enjoying my rugby, playing centre for the Wits Under-19 side. Eight of us were chosen to play for the Transvaal team, namely John Heyns, who was also the captain, Jan Kruger, Mike Wellsted, Ray Hanna, Don Mulinder, Vernon Sachs, Cornelius Findlay and me.

Before long, it was cricket again. For a period during the 1958/9 season, I kept wicket for Wits and, during a match against Wanderers, I managed to stump the great Johnny Waite, the Springbok wicketkeeper, for a duck. I enjoyed my work behind the stumps, but I missed my bowling too much and it was not long before I gave up the gloves and bowled again.

Next rugby season, I was made captain of the Under-19 side and we had a dream season with a great 26-0 win over Airways and notable victories over Cape Town and Potchefstroom. Once again, eight of us were chosen for the Transvaal Under-20s: Alan Menter, Peter Enslin, Peter Mabbett, Mike Collins, Anthony Marsh, Tuttie Fisher, me and, last but not least, the young Frederik van Zyl Slabbert, who in years to come became my political mentor.

Once again, the rugby season flowed into the cricket season with scarcely time to draw breath, and I opened my batting account with a century against Pirates followed by 107 against a Southern Suburbs side that included Ken Walker and Cyril Tayfield. It was downhill after that, but I still managed to top the batting averages, scoring 733 runs at an average of 29.32. That wasn't good enough, but my bowling was coming along and I managed to get a hat trick against Balfour Park towards the end of the season.

Representative honours were starting to come my way. First, I was included in the South African University XI. We played just one game, against Transvaal, and lost by an innings. Neil Adcock, Mike McCauley and Hugh Tayfield were in the provincial side and I was fortunate to make 56 in 88 minutes. Next, it was the Transvaal selectors who called, asking me to play for the provincial B side. I managed to score 72 on my debut, against Griqualand West.

These were happy, hectic days.

With a bit of luck, insofar as I usually found myself in the right place at the right time, I continued to move up the ladder in cricket and rugby. The year 1960 turned out to be the big breakthrough year for me, when I was selected to make my debut for both the Transvaal rugby team and the Transvaal cricket team.

I won my provincial cap for rugby first, and had the greatest good fortune to be named in the Transvaal team to play against the touring All Blacks at Ellis Park. That afternoon turned out to a major highlight of my brief provincial rugby career.

There was a huge crowd at the old Ellis Park stadium, which was nothing like the luxurious, modern stadium we know today. In those days, the crowds used to sit on the Quinn's bakery building and many temporary stands were built to accommodate as many as 100,000 fans at major matches. It was a full house.

My midfield partner in the Vaal team was Mike Antelme, and he usually had some chirp or other during a game. Halfway through the match against New Zealand, our jerseys were still pristine white with one red horizontal stripe because the All Black forwards were on top and our backline had hardly touched the ball.

Half-time came and went, and the pattern of play remained just about the same. Early in the second half, the All Blacks won a scrum and, as we moved up in defence, Terry Lineen tried to chip the ball over our heads. I jumped up and caught the ball. It was a fantastic moment for me, but the joy didn't last. The next moment, I was caught in mid-air by what seemed to be an entire posse of loose forwards, and they proceeded to carry me and the ball from our 25-yard line to just in front of our line. There, I was unceremoniously dumped on the ground.

My joy had quickly turned to embarrassment and, feeling as if I should somehow defend my honour, I turned around to find the substantial figure of Colin 'Pinetree' Meads lying beside me. Without thinking, I pulled back my right arm ready to strike.

"Don't!" said the legendary All Black.

So I didn't.

I was the laughing stock of the entire Transvaal team after the game, and it must have looked odd to see this little squirt of a student attempting to re-arrange the facial features of so great a rugby man. Mind you, I felt grateful for 'Pinetree' for stopping me from doing something that would have got me into trouble, if not from the referee, then certainly from Colin himself. He was a true gentleman of rugby, the like of which the game lacks today.

Transvaal were well beaten that afternoon, by 19-13, and we had taken the field with twelve full Springboks in the side. Nonetheless, for me, it had been a privilege to be involved. Sport was affording me the kind of opportunities that most South Africans of my age could only dream about, and I will always be grateful.

In 1961 I was chosen to join an invitation cricket team called the Fezelas, which was preparing to tour England. The team was created by a retired sugar cane planter from Durban by the name of Ted Murphy, and was conceived to give experience to young players with the potential to, one day, represent South Africa.

It was a strong team, but that message had not reached our English hosts, who had arranged for us to play sides that seemed considerably weaker than we were. The word 'fezela' means scorpion in Zulu, and I remember 'Uncle Ted', as we all knew him, saying he wanted us to provide a sting in the tail, and surprise the Englishmen who underrated the strength of South African cricket.

Ted Murphy probably contributed around R20,000 to fund the tour, joining the ranks of other generous men who had served as benefactors of South African cricket: people like Wilf Isaacs, whose team used to give youngsters an early taste of top class cricket.

It was a hugely successful tour. Two members of the squad, Roy MacLean and Chris Burger, were already Springbok cricketers, but of the other twelve players in that Fezelas squad, no fewer than seven – Dennis Lindsay, Colin Bland, Peter Pollock, Jackie Botten, Peter van der Merwe, Kim Elgie and me – learned, matured and later played Test cricket for South Africa.

Each of us owed a great debt to 'Uncle Ted'. He was a wonderful gentleman, and we were all very proud to wear the blue and black cap with a scorpion on the crest.

Our itinerary based us in the midlands, with other matches in the south of England and even one in Scotland. When we were not playing, we either played proper practice matches organised by Roy MacLean, a man who was revered for his swash-buckling approach to the game, or we did fitness work arranged by Colin Bland, whose enthusiasm rubbed off on the rest of us. We were young, and keen, so proud to be playing in England and we were a very happy bunch. It was a great tour.

I have been asked about chirping, or sledging, in those days and I have to say that, at the time, most of us didn't really know what that was. In 1961, I don't think the practice had arrived in South Africa, but it didn't take long for us to learn the art of rattling the opposition from our English hosts. However, in contrast to modern practice, our chirping tended to be amusing and witty, rather than personal and nasty.

We learned on the field, and off the field as well. After a game at Blackheath CC, in southeast London, we were invited to watch a show at Raymond's Revue Bar in Soho. This was, in every sense of the word, an eye-opener for me, aged 20 and seeing all those girls removing their clothes. Some of them performed belly dances and others stripped completely. After a while, the music suddenly changed and, as if by magic, all the enormously breasted women disappeared from the stage and were replaced by what I reckoned were more reasonably sized, 'real' women. These smaller girls were greeted by more claps and wolf whistles.

There seemed to be strip clubs wherever we went, and we soon developed an uncanny knack of finding them. There was even one with a sign on the door that read: 'Come in and paint the nude… watch the artists at work'. Unable to resist, we wandered inside and discovered a naked lady with huge breasts being painted with large brushes. Anyone could grab a pot of paint and a brush, and start slopping the stuff all over her.

She looked a mess at the end of the evening, but we had all paid for the privilege, so I suppose she was rewarded. Personally, I thought it was all a bit odd and decided that, as the British say, we had been 'had'. While the first few strip clubs were fun, the consensus emerged that more was not better and that we should concentrate on cricket in England, rather than more clubs. All in all, it had been an experience, but I don't think it improved me.

We also took in the more conventional sights of London, including the Changing of the Guard at Buckingham Palace and the Whispering Gallery in St Paul's Cathedral. Our visit to the Tower of London was popular as well.

One evening, the touring group was invited to have drinks and some substantial snacks at the Overseas Visitors Club. I chose to leave relatively early, planning to walk across Hyde Park on my way back to our hotel in Bayswater. But it was pitch dark and, before long I found myself ankle deep in the Serpentine lake. I was mercilessly mocked, but it was all fun.

We played one match in Portsmouth against the Combined Services. After the match we were taken to the place where it had been arranged for us to spend the night. In the Army and the Royal Air Force, these officers' barracks are known as the Mess, but the Fezelas were being hosted by the Royal Navy, so we headed to the officers' accommodation known as the Wardroom.

Each young South African cricketer was allocated a 'batman' for the duration of our stay. This sounded intriguing, but I hadn't a clue what they were talking about until a smiling old man appeared at the door of my room. He was grey, wizened and well into his seventies. He could have been not even my father, but my grandfather.

"May I have your clothes to wash for the morning, Sir?" he asked, and I was happy to oblige. He also took my shoes. When I woke up early the next day, I discovered that the clothes were perfectly pressed, and the shoes were shining like new pins.

The man then appeared as I arrived for breakfast, laid out a newspaper on the table before me and enquired whether I would like my eggs sunny side up or any other way. He brought it all to me, together with hot toast and marmalade.

It transpired that every member of the team we had played the previous day had been an officer, and each of them had their own batman, so they gave us the same treatment.

However, there was one difference. We noticed that when the British naval officers arrived for breakfast, their batmen had gone to the trouble of actually ironing their newspapers, so the crease would be in precisely the right place. We could hardly believe it: an ironed newspaper! We had travelled six thousand miles to see things we'd never even imagined. Heavens, what a country!

Incidentally, the 1961 Fezelas managed to win each of the 21 matches we played on tour, but all we heard when we got back home was that our record didn't mean anything because the opposition was supposedly so weak.

The argument was settled soon afterwards, when the Fezelas played a game against the Springbok team. I'm pleased to say we defeated the Boks, and no more was said.

The following weekend I was back in my rugby boots, getting ready to play for Wits in the annual intervarsity match against the University of Pretoria at Loftus Versfeld. Tukkies, as the UP team is known, were

That's me, the third from the left, middle row, the blonde baby face of my house rugby team at Pretoria Boys High, 1956

All aboard for the Boys High rugby tour to White River; that's me, the 'four-eyes'

odds-on favourites to win but, to general amazement, we tackled all afternoon, rode our luck and emerged with a fantastic 16-5 victory. It was
my best twenty-first birthday present.

I was beginning to wonder how long I could keep playing both sports,
juggling the increasingly demanding time commitments of provincial
rugby and provincial cricket.

After much soul searching, I made my decision in April 1962. Some
people were advising me to stop playing rugby there and then, and concentrate on the cricket, but I decided to play just one more rugby season,
largely because the British and Irish Lions were scheduled to tour South
Africa that year and I relished the chance of playing against them.

My opportunity came when I was included in the Northern Universi-
ties side to play the Lions in the town of Springs, east of Johannesburg.
We were a bunch of nervous students and before the game Dr Danie
Craven arrived in our changing room.

He was a legend in the game, and we were all in awe of a man who had
played for South Africa as scrumhalf of the 1937 Invincibles team that
won in New Zealand, who had coached the team, managed the team and
been President of the South African Rugby Board since 1957. The room
fell silent when he walked in, and everybody looked towards him.

"Listen," he said, with the hint of a smile and a glimmer in his eye. "If
you don't do better than the last northern universities team, then you
won't play a touring side again."

Then, he walked around the changing room, punching each and every
player on the shoulder, saying: "And if you don't play well, you're going
to get more of this."

Doc was a famous motivator, and we managed to hold our own that
day against the Lions. I had always enjoyed watching their backs in full
flow, particularly the Welshmen. Their approach was so different. There
was a saying at the time that the Lions played rugby to get fit, while
South Africans got fit to play rugby, and there is no doubt that they did
have a more Corinthian attitude to the game. It was physical and serious for us. I thought their flyhalf, Richard Sharp, was a really wonderful
player, but injury seemed to have taken the wind out of his sails.

The press had also written a lot about Alan Jones, the magical Lions centre, and it didn't take long for me to know exactly what they were talking about. Early in the match, Jones received the ball and I moved up to tackle him. He did this deft little sidestep to the right and, in front of 30,000 people, I fell flat on my face.

Our fullback managed to tackle him but, as I was feeling sorry for myself, my centre partner came running past, and said: "You've got to watch these *okes* (guys), Eddie, because they are ambidextrous in both feet."

I recovered my composure and played my part in securing a 6-6 draw, which might have been better if we hadn't missed three straightforward penalties. After the game, some of the Lions were kind enough to say I was one of the best centres they had played against on their tour. That kind of comment was an encouragement, but I stuck by my decision to stop playing rugby at the end of the 1962 season, at the age of 22.

Over the years, I have often wondered what might have happened if I continued playing rugby. Would I have played for the Springboks? Maybe. I will never know, but I do think my chances would have been enhanced if I had been an Afrikaner. The reality in the 1960s was that South African rugby was generally dominated by Afrikaans-speakers, and, in terms of getting selected in the various representative teams, I knew it was never going to be easy for an English-speaking centre like me. I'm not saying it was impossible, but it would never be easy.

Anyway, that didn't matter any more. From September 1962, I had decided cricket was going to be my game.

Chapter Four – Learning Days

One mark of a successful sportsman or woman is a capacity to learn from every experience and every situation. Nobody ever 'knows it all' and, so long as an individual is humble enough to keep his eyes and his mind open, he will continue learning and improving. Even if he is generally regarded as one of the best batsmen or bowlers in the world, he can still learn.

I started learning the game of cricket in the best possible place, in the back yard with my father and older brother. We used to play at every free moment of the day, and that is where I was taught the basic skills of batting, bowling and fielding.

There were mishaps in the back yard, when one of my pull shots dislodged the bowl of custard my mother was carrying to the table for our Sunday lunch, and when our straight drives decapitated the cauliflowers in my father's vegetable patch (we used to balance them back on their stalks, and, for as long as I can remember, Pops used to blame the cutworms).

Various coaches helped and inspired me, first at primary school and then at secondary school, enabling me to reach a point in the early 1960s where it seemed as though, with a bit of luck, I could make something of a cricket career at the highest level.

I kept learning when I played for Wits University, kept learning through age-group teams, and kept learning when I was selected for Transvaal. By the start of 1963, having finally made the decision to stop playing rugby, I decided to embark upon the next stage of my cricketing education.

At the age of 24, I headed to a tough school, the Lancashire leagues. This was club cricket played in and around the cities of Manchester, Preston and Liverpool in the north-west of England. I had spoken to many senior South African cricketers who had travelled to play in the Lancashire Leagues: some came home with horror stories but without exception, they said it was the place to learn the ins and outs of the game.

They were 100 per cent right.

It was arranged for me to play a season for Accrington Cricket Club and I duly arrived in April 1964. In those days, the Lancashire leagues were full of great players, like Ian Galash, of Australia, Charlie Griffiths and Roy Gilchrist from the West Indies, Akram Elahi from Pakistan and, of course, a number of English Test players who somehow found their way 'up north' to supplement their salaries.

The standard of cricket was exceptionally high, and matches were well attended. The clubs actively marketed themselves, advertising upcoming matches with billboards that appeared on lamp posts in towns across the county. And they didn't advertise 'Burnley vs. Accrington': they would promote the so-called big names and bill the match as 'Charlie Griffiths, West Indies vs. Eddie Barlow, South Africa'.

With all the undertones of a contest like that in the mid-1960s, the spectators were soon rolling up to see what would happen. In fact, Charlie gave me a few problems that season.

First we played at Burnley, and I was out cheaply in the first innings, clean-bowled by his first ball. In the second innings, the great West Indian bowled me for a golden duck. It was a terrible moment and I still recall hearing the ball clatter into my stumps, and turning to see all three ripped out of the ground.

Things didn't get much better for me when they came to play at Accrington a couple of months later. Charlie bowled a searing, seriously quick yorker that struck me on the instep, and forced me to leave the field during the first innings. I recovered to bat in the second innings, but was lbw Griffiths for not many. As I made my way back to the pavilion, someone shouted: "That was a load of *roobish*, Barlow."

It was the ultimate insult in Lancashire, and I had arrived thinking I was quite a respectable player. Anyway, I took it on the chin. Even on the tough days, I managed to keep learning.

On another occasion, the heavens opened and the entire north of England seemed to disappear under water. Still, the match started on time and, as anybody who has seen a fielding team struggle to bowl with a wet ball will understand, we were soon facing serious problems.

It was so wet that, when the opposing batsmen hit the ball into the outfield, it would roll over the wet grass and through puddles, leaving a trail of spray in its wake. At Accrington, we called this 'feathering', because it looked like the comb on a cockerel's head. It wasn't much fun but, on days like this, when the umpires kept us out there, we became accustomed to looking for every available piece of cloth, whether it was a shirt, a towel or whatever to dry the ball and try to get some kind of grip.

We were struggling in this particular match and our groundsman, 'Owd Fred', as he was known to all, decided he was going to do his bit for the team. So he walked out to the wicket, carrying a 25-litre bucket of sawdust. I had no idea what he was doing because I hadn't called for any sawdust, and there were no damp areas that needed any. As he arrived, I was more interested in trying to push the sodden ball deeper and deeper into my pocket, trying to soak up some of the moisture and get it dry.

"What's that for?" I asked, as he reached me.

"Just take some," Owd Fred said, winking.

"Why?" I asked, still not seeing the point.

"Just take some," he repeated, still winking.

I reached down into the bucket, and, buried deep down in the sawdust, I felt the shape of a cricket ball tucked away at the bottom. It was bone dry.

"Hey, Fred, what's this for?" I asked.

"Shut up," he snapped. "Just swap that one for the wet one, and get some wickets."

I did as I was told, and we were soon moving along quite merrily, making inroads into the opposition's batting order. Fred sat and watched, smiling, innocent as a lamb. We won the game, and there was a collection among the crowd, which was shared between the bowlers and Fred in the local pub.

Rain rarely stopped play in those days. I remember driving to one game, which didn't seem to have a hope of starting because of the weather. The heavens had opened and, when we arrived at the ground, the grass was covered with snow-white hailstones. I joined my mates in the changing room, and we were just thinking about leaving when suddenly there was a loud banging on the door.

"*Coom owt 'n play, ye boogers*," a broad Lancashire voice shouted out. We could not turn down an invitation like that and, in steady drizzle, among puddles, the match started on time.

I enjoyed my season with Accrington, but the highlight of the year was getting married to Helen. We had met at Wits, and tended to turn up at the same social events that peppered the university calendar. We both planned to become teachers, an ambition that Helen, unlike me, fulfilled. I remember our geography lectures so well. Helen and her friend Jenny Webster used to sit in front of me and my mate Pete Eedes. Amazingly, as it turned out, I married Helen, and Pete married Jenny.

Helen was travelling around Europe that year, and we agreed that she would come to England while I was at Accrington. Some of her relations lived near Winchester, so we arranged to get married in a lovely little church called St Cross, in a village called Owlesbury, pronounced Usselberry. Everything was arranged.

We planned to spend our honeymoon in Scotland, and drove north in my little minivan, which just about did the job apart from one afternoon when it kept flooding and stalling during a downpour on the A74. Our first night was spent in a bed and breakfast outside Glasgow, which turned out to be a bit ropey but the lack of comfort was compensated for by a first class breakfast. That became the pattern of the week – dodgy hotels and magnificent breakfasts – and we had a very happy time.

Helen stayed with me for the rest of the season in Lancashire and, when it was over in September, we returned to Johannesburg and the prospect of a new life in the Eastern Cape.

It's strange how things just seem to happen. Some people reckoned my decision to leave Johannesburg and move to Port Elizabeth was motivated purely by a desire to be the captain of a provincial cricket team. That is just not true. That was the last thing on my mind, and there was never a great plan.

The rather more mundane truth is that I needed a job and, one afternoon after cricket practice, I was talking to an old timer who had worked for SA Breweries. I mentioned I was looking for work, and he said he knew some people at SAB. He suggested he give them a call, and promised to let me know.

Sure enough, he phoned the next day, and an interview followed. I was duly employed as a salesman for the SA Breweries with an immediate transfer to the friendly city of Port Elizabeth.

SAB seemed to have a policy of employing sportsmen, because they believed well known names would help sell their products, Castle Lager and Lion Lager. For many sportsmen of my era, it was the dream job. Breweries were very understanding about playing commitments, letting us come and go as necessary, but they also provided excellent training and the prospect of a genuine career after sport.

Helen and I decided to seize the opportunity and we settled quickly in Port Elizabeth, where our son Craig was born. I began to play for Eastern Province and, after a few matches, was invited to captain the team. It was not a plan. Captaincy had never been something I craved. You often hear youngsters saying their ambition is to grow up and captain their country, but that was never on my mind. I just wanted to play.

Anyway, the opportunity came, and I accepted. Even in those days, I had some ideas about how to prepare and train a team, and I was eager to put them into practice. A classy young batsman called Graeme Pollock had emerged as the star of the EP team in those days, and we were a decent side.

In all, Helen and I spent three years in the Eastern Cape, and it was one of the most enjoyable periods of my life. The local cricket community was among the most knowledgeable in South Africa, and we enjoyed spending time with the Eastern Cape farmers. These old established families were mostly descended from the 1820 Settlers who arrived from England to make new lives in Africa, and we loved hearing all the old stories about the various battles and how their ancestors had tamed the land.

Most of these farmers loved their sport, especially cricket, and their enthusiasm was so great that they launched their own annual cricket festival, known as the 'Pineapple Week'. Every town in the area used to get involved, and top cricketers came from around the province to play at packed grounds.

One or other young player always seemed to emerge as the star of the week, and the debates would rage endlessly about whether this young-ster or that youngster would become the next superstar of South African cricket. As the evenings wore on, the discussions would become more and more animated until, more often than not, everybody would turn to me and ask for my verdict.

This kind of situation put me in a tight spot but it didn't take long for me to develop a stock response that would keep me out of trouble. I used to take a deep breath and say: "Well, they're both good players and there's no doubt they could both play for EP but, all I know for sure is that nobody will ever be as good as Graeme Pollock". Everybody would nod in eager agreement – in EP, at that time, it was impossible to disa-gree – and I had got myself off the hook.

These farmers were wonderful people, and we kept in touch with many of them for many years. I remember they used to set off on these great hunting expeditions and, while that was never my thing, we always returned home with several weeks' supply of excellent venison and bil-tong.

In the Eastern Cape there was no shortage of outstanding schools which produced tough, resourceful and uncompromising children, many of whom grew up to play provincial sport. Life was straightforward and simple at that time. If a family was struggling to pay the school fees, Dad would go out and shoot a kudu and take it to the butcher to raise some cash. We lived in that kind of community, and I loved it.

The farmers were great jokers. In those days, the farms had outside loos, holes in the ground known as 'the long drop'. There was a tin shack that surrounded the long drop, and it made an ideal shooting target be-cause it made a very pleasing noise when the bullets bounced off the corrugated iron.

The kids knew all about this, and they used to wait until an unsuspecting visitor had gone inside. They would then shoot a bullet or two at the shack. Needless to say, the occupant would clamber out of there as quickly as he could get his trousers up, amid much hilarity from the audience.

The farmers were always up to something. During one Test against Australia at St George's Park in Port Elizabeth, I met up with the Pohl brothers, who hailed from Grahamstown. They were passionate about cricket and wanted South Africa to do well, and I remember them saying they would give each of us R200 every time we hit an Aussie with a bouncer. That was a lot of money in those days.

We laughed, but didn't take them too seriously, at least not until the start of the game when we noticed the Pohls had taken their seats right on the boundary. They remained there for the rest of the day, and never stopped shouting for us to bowl faster and hit our targets.

My life took another turn in 1967 when I attended a sales conference between some representatives of SA Breweries and the Stellenbosch Farmers Winery (SFW). During the meeting I was handed a note that read: 'Why don't you come and live among the Lieberstein bushes in the Cape?' The paper was signed by Piet Roussouw, from SFW. I arranged to meet him later that day and he offered me a job as SFW's Area Sales Manager in the Western Cape. The opportunity came out of the blue, but it seemed attractive.

I later discovered Piet had been asked by his boss at SFW, Wally Mitchell, to recruit some cricketers who would improve the SFW side, and maybe also play for a struggling Western Province team. Piet had seen me at the sales conference and, it seemed, made his move on the spur of the moment, without even consulting Wally. This led to what they call an animated exchange the next day at the office.

Wally asked: "What have you done? Who is this guy?"

"Edgar John Barlow," Piet replied.

Wide-eyed Wally asked: "What post have you offered him?"

"Area Sales Manager"

"OK, fine."

I discussed the prospect with Helen, and we both decided a move to the Cape would suit us very well. Once again, the cricket rumour mill moved into action, and it was even reported that I had been tempted to move to the Cape by the offer of a house. That was not strictly true.

In those innocent days, there were no signed contracts or negotiated benefits for cricketers, but this is what happened: Helen and I arranged to visit Stellenbosch, where we met Wally Mitchell and had a look around. Wally and his fellow directors had really put SFW on the map, and we were impressed not only by what they has achieved but also by their future plans. Luckily, our visit coincided with the running of the Metropolitan Handicap, the biggest occasion in the Cape season, and Wally owned a horse called William Penn, who was running in an earlier race. He invited us to join him at the Kenilworth racecourse for the big day.

During lunch Wally took a call from his trainer, who said the horse was in fine fettle and stood an excellent chance. Wally turned to Helen and said: "The odds on that horse are 66/1, and I will put R100 on him for you." Needless to say, the horse galloped to victory, and the winnings enabled us to put a deposit on a particular house that we happened to have seen on the hill at Union Park, Stellenbosch.

I got stuck into the challenge of helping the SFW cricket team and, luckily, discovered one of my teammates was Hylton Ackerman. 'Dutchman' became one of my best mates in the game, and there was never a dull moment when he was around.

I remember the day when we decided to take the guys on a training run at Craven's Hill behind the cricket oval at the University. The paths had been laid out by Doc Craven, himself, to train the rugby players. Cricketers didn't usually do this kind of thing, but we all set off at the double.

Never too keen on training, Dutchman was jogging along at the back of the group. It was getting dark when we began the descent and, as we reached the bottom, we heard this strange plaintive cry from above. Baboons were barking in the hills, but the noise didn't sound like one of them. It was Dutchman: some of us went back up the mountain and heard him explain how he had taken a wrong turn.

Helen and I enjoyed our years in Stellenbosch, working for SFW and playing cricket. The town was, first and foremost, a rugby stronghold, and we spent many happy afternoons watching Maties, the University first XV, play at the Danie Craven stadium. The 'Doc' was always around, and his presence set the tone.

I was invited to play for the Stellenbosch University cricket club, and duly turned up to discover the team included Morné du Plessis, later to become Springbok rugby captain, Andre Bruyns, a young all-rounder called Mike Procter, and Dave McKay, who later owned the Constantia Uitsig restaurant and wine estate.

They were a great bunch. Andre in particular, became a firm friend and fellow *joller*, whose escapades were always a source of amusement on and off the field. There was once a luncheon to mark the launch of a new SFW product, and we were standing around when the proprietor of a local club arrived with his extremely attractive wife. She proceeded to sit in the empty seat beside me, prompting my mate Andre to grab the empty seat across the table, a little too quickly for my liking.

Next, I felt a slight nudge on my ankle, followed by the slow, gentle rubbing of a foot up and down my right leg. I quickly realised it was Andre, who thought he had found the lady's leg. I said nothing. After a while, I decided to liven things up a bit, so I put my hand under the table, stuck it up his trouser leg and started rubbing his calf. His face lit up like a child's at Christmas.

A few minutes later I thought I would go a little further, so I stretched down, grabbed his ankle with both hands and gave it a tug. Well, in all the excitement, Don Juan slipped off his chair and disappeared under the table. It was a lovely moment.

I also played for the SFW cricket XI, although, once I was playing for South Africa, I wasn't always welcome in that kind of social match. One day, playing for SFW in Paarl, an umpire called 'Blackie' Swart gave me out in the second over, lbw to a ball that hit me very high on the thigh, and told our captain matter-of-factly: "Broer Piet, you cannot bring Eddie to play against us here, so I have given him out lbw."

On another occasion we were playing at Langebaan, a small fishing village up the west coast from Cape Town. This was the place where Al-

Ian Lamb, the South African born England batsman, grew up when his father was Commander of the local SA Air Force base.

There was a gale blowing. We fielded first and, every time somebody was bowled, we heard a peculiar tinkling noise from the wickets. It took us a while to realise that the local club had invested in a pair of aluminium bails, which were heavy enough to stay in place on the stumps, even in the strong wind.

At any rate, these bails tinkled regularly through their innings and, when we had knocked off the runs, we were packing up our kit and getting ready for the long drive back to Stellenbosch. Their club secretary suddenly appeared. He was angry. "Can't you see how many people have come to watch you play?" he asked. "We must play a few more overs, and give them more entertainment. If you don't mind, I will decide when you leave." He was red-faced and strong, and we did as we were told.

There was a great spirit within the SFW club, and at one stage we decided a piece of waste ground at the back of the company headquarters would make an ideal cricket pitch. Everybody was enthusiastic, and we all got stuck in to the task of creating a new field from nothing.

We dug a long trench and hurled in all the broken glass and river stones we could find to make a strong foundation for the pitch. We then covered it with some high quality clay from a little place called Koelenhof, just down the road. The wicket turned out to be a belter, and in later years it hosted regular provincial matches. In fact, I'm proud to say the SFW ground is still going strong today.

I enjoyed my work as well. My beat was the Observatory and Salt River districts of Cape Town. 'Obs', as it is known, had not been 'discovered' by the fashionable estate agents in those days, but it was a busy trading area and proved a good place to operate. The territory suited me well because all the clients were keen on sport. I used to arrive at their offices in my white Valiant car, and spend many hours discussing the pros and cons of every rugby and cricket team in South Africa, before selling the odd bottle of wine.

At one stage, the SFW marketing department decided to launch a new product called Golden Mustang. They planned a big sales drive, and purchased two new Golden Mustang sports cars, which were going to be paraded through the various 'likker' outlets that seemed likely to sell this kind of product.

That was not all. There was a third car in the cavalcade, pulling a horsebox containing two palomino horses. At various venues, sales reps like me were expected to take the horses out and ride them around outside the sales outlet. It was a lot of fun, especially for the children who always seemed to gather around whenever we started our show, even though they were not exactly the target market for alcohol.

We spent a very happy month taking this performance all over the country, and everything went well until we reached Kimberley. I was riding one of the horses through the township of Galashewe when I heard some serious barking. A growling Alsatian appeared, and bit my horse high up on its rump. The palomino gave a snort, bucked and threw me backwards, leaving me sitting in the dust.

Three of my colleagues, dressed up like cowboys, were perched on the back of a truck, driving behind. They had seen my fall, and thought it was hilarious. So did the driver of their truck, who laughed so hard that his foot slipped onto the accelerator. The truck shot forward like a rocket, and my three mates were thrown off the back, landing beside me in the dust. I enjoyed the last laugh.

Thankfully, the parades generally went well and Golden Mustang was a huge success.

Cavorting around as a cowboy to sell alcohol may have seemed an unlikely activity for an established Test cricketer, which by that time I had become, but cricket was not a living in those days, and we all had to work. I was happy at SFW, and enjoyed being a member of the sales team.

Through the 1960s my cricketing exploits meant I became increasingly well known in South Africa and, when that happens to someone, I was starting to realise that they tend to get put in a box. The public read about you, or watch you play, and some sort of reputation develops.

In those days, I was generally regarded as an energetic competitor, bustling around, always getting involved in something or other. This was thought to be a positive thing, but some people also began to regard me as being controversial. I think this tag was created by one or two notable incidents and, for better or worse, it stayed with me throughout most of my career. The label on my box read 'controversial'.

One of these incidents occurred at the annual banquet held by the Rand Sportswriters in Johannesburg. Each year the journalists voted for their Sportsman of the Year and on this particular occasion, it seemed the two main candidates were De Villiers Lamprecht, the middle-distance athlete, and me.

As the evening progressed, I became aware of some muttered whispering to the effect that I was going to win the award only because there were more English-speaking than Afrikaans-speaking journalists, and they would all vote for me. I couldn't stand that kind of thing, and became increasingly annoyed.

The announcement was duly made that I had won, and I went up to collect the trophy and a watch. However, when I returned to my seat, I was so irritated by continuing talk of the English-Afrikaans divisions that, right there and then, I decided I would not accept the award.

So I marched up to the main table, handed the trophy and the watch back to the judges, and offered a few choice words about the suggestions that people were only voting for me because I was an English-speaker. I said I didn't want anything to do with something that seemed so ridden with division and hatred.

People were shocked, and some of my friends told me just to keep quiet and accept the award, but it was a matter of principle for me. Next day, the newspapers ran comprehensive accounts of my behaviour, very few of them flattering, but I didn't mind.

If doing what I believed was right meant some people thought I was 'controversial', then I had to accept that. Over the years that followed, I made a point of declining every invitation to the Rand Sportswriters' banquet. I wanted nothing to do with it.

Chapter Five – Test Days (1961-64)

The South African cricket team played a total of 30 official Test matches during the 1960s, starting with the five-Test home series against New Zealand in 1961/2, and finishing with the four home Tests against Bill Lawry's Australians in 1969/70. I was fortunate to be involved in the team throughout this period, before the curtain of exclusion fell and prompted 22 years of official isolation.

It had always been my ambition to represent my country, either at cricket or rugby, in fact at anything, and I can still vividly recall the precise moment of my selection.

I was with the Transvaal team, and we happened to be in the city of Bulwayo, playing the team then known as Rhodesia. Someone had been listening to the radio, and they walked into the sitting room of our hotel and told me I was in the South African side to play New Zealand in the first Test at Kingsmead, Durban.

There had been some talk that I might be in contention for a place, but the news was still a huge surprise. All I could think about was making the most of the opportunity: not being just a member of the South African cricket team, but being a member of a South African cricket team that actually won Tests.

As soon as we returned to Johannesburg, I went to see a man called Algy Frames, who was the secretary of the South African Cricket Union in those days. I had to collect a particularly precious piece of dark green fabric and then arrange to have my Springbok blazer made up by a tailor. That was the way things were done back then. I'm not sure what the modern players would have made of that kind of thing.

So I collected the fabric from Mr. Frames and, travelling on my Vespa scooter, made my way to Patel Bros in Fordsburg, west of the city centre. The tailors knew me well, and seemed just as excited as I was about the task of cutting and sewing my first Springbok cricket blazer.

The only other item of kit provided by SACU was the cap, and this was duly presented to me on the first day of the first Test against New Zealand in Durban. In fact, there were seven new caps that bright morning in early November 1961, and the day seemed to represent something of a new dawn.

The new boys were Ken Walter, Colin Bland, Peter Pollock, Kim Elgie, Harry Bromfield, Godfrey 'Goofy' Lawrence and me, and we relied heavily on the guidance and experience of the four more experienced members of the team: captain Derrick 'Jackie' McGlew, Johnny Waite, Roy McLean and Sid O'Lin.

I remember Sid had a tremendous sense of humour. He was always great value in the changing room, and he loved to entertain the crowd. In one match the batsman hit a skier towards him in the outfield. As the ball dropped towards him, he prepared to take the catch by theatrically holding up his hands, then dropping to one knee, then to both knees... but the ball was dragged away by a gust of wind and it fell to ground three feet in front of him. The crowd laughed, but Hugh Tayfield, the bowler, was not amused.

Jackie McGlew was an exceptionally brave and gutsy cricketer, but he was never the type of captain for the big team talk, so, with no such thing as a coach telling players what to do, each of us was pretty much left on our own to practise, prepare and motivate ourselves exactly as we wanted. It's not an exaggeration to say that, for the most part, we pretty much turned up and got on with the game.

It wasn't an easy time for Jackie, because he had the task of moulding a team from a handful of experienced Test players and all the new lads. I sometimes felt that, as youngsters, we were too brash and confident for our skipper. We thought we could take everything in our stride, and we were wrong.

Personally, I was soon put in my place. The mood and intensity of Test cricket was unlike anything I had ever experienced, and, quite literally, it stunned me. We batted first and, opening the innings with Jackie, I was overcome by nerves and started slashing at anything and everything.

People couldn't understand what I was doing, and I didn't have a decent explanation. If any young player asks me what to expect on his Test debut, I always tell him to expect something he has never felt at any other level of the game. You have to respect the environment and keep calm.

Unsurprisingly, I was out cheaply in both innings, but Peter Pollock bowled magnificently, and we were very relieved to win the first Test of the five-match series by just 30 runs.

Things went slightly better for me in the second Test, and I managed to score 47 in the first innings and 45 in the second. John Reid was the captain of New Zealand, and I was flattered when he put a fielder between the slips and third man specially to stop me scoring runs from my trademark flying late-cut.

Even so, I was still going for my strokes, and I was keenly aware that more than a few wise heads were watching me, shaking their heads and wondering what on earth I was doing. At least I had scored a few runs and not disgraced myself. The Test ended in a draw, after almost a day and half was lost to rain.

The third Test was played at Newlands and, as I finally started to settle into the rhythm of Test cricket, the series began to take off. Peter Pollock had bowled a few bouncers at the Kiwi tail-enders at the end of the second Test and the New Zealanders were not at all pleased. Their fast bowler Gary Bartlett launched the Cape Town Test with a barrage of bumpers. He just didn't stop. Jackie McGlew was furious and tempers were flaring. If anybody reckons Test cricket was a tea party in the 1960s, they should have been there.

Some of our players started to suggest Bartlett was a 'chucker', but the umpires never called him. Nothing was said officially because, in those days, we just had a grumble and got on with the game.

I managed to score 51 at Newlands, but we lost the match by 72 runs. Some peopled thought we had been rattled by the aggressive approach of the New Zealanders, so, somewhat upset, we headed to the fourth Test in Johannesburg with the series level at 1-1. Relations were deteriorating.

Jackie was not a man to stand back. He said he wanted to meet fire with fire, and insisted two more fast bowlers, Neil Adcock and Peter Heine, should be called into our team. They duly arrived, and joined the battle. It was nothing less. To say the air turned blue would be an understatement.

Peter Heine was a real trouper, and he launched his counter attack on John Reid and the New Zealanders with gusto. He gave everything, not holding anything back. The umpires tended not to get involved in this type of situation, preferring to let the players sort things out for themselves.

Well, over by over, bouncer by bouncer, threat by threat, the situation escalated. I was amazed at what was going on. Peter didn't back down, but John Reid was no shrinking violet either. A real tough customer, he was the glue that held the New Zealand team together and I admired that.

We won the Test by 51 runs, but everybody was talking about the battle between Peter and Reid. To our great disappointment, the South African press seemed to take Reid's side. They hammered Peter, creating the general atmosphere that led to him being dropped from our side for the last Test. That decision was completely unfair, and did nothing to improve relations between the sides.

There was also some excellent cricket. Colin Bland had produced a brilliant performance in the field at the Wanderers. He was my kind of cricketer, a true fitness fanatic in a period when anybody who looked as though they might break out into a sweat was labelled a 'freak'. He understood that his fitness and agility were crucial to his excellence in the field, and the catch he took to dismiss John Reid was fantastic. Given everything else that was going on, it was a popular wicket for his teammates, and people still talk about it today.

Colin was the greatest fielder I have ever seen, with only Jonty Rhodes bearing any comparison.

So we took a 2-1 lead into the final Test at St George's Park in Port Elizabeth, and blew it. New Zealand won the match and managed to square the series. It's true we were missing a few players who were injured, and we may have been distracted by the sledging and animosity between the sides but, whatever the case, John Reid had done a great job for his side. With hindsight, he probably won the psychological war.

The result was bitterly disappointing for the older players in our team, who had desperately wanted to win their last series before they retired, but the drawn series did provide a valuable lesson for us, the younger members of the side... specifically that Test cricket is a tough environment, where success is secured not only by a full-blooded determination to win, but also by keeping a cool head.

South Africa didn't play another Test for two years after the home series against New Zealand. It seems to surprise some people, but in the entire history of Springbok cricket from its inception until the start of isolation, we only ever played three other countries: England, Australia and New Zealand. The other cricketing countries, like the West Indies, India and Pakistan, wanted nothing to do with the country of apartheid and, I suppose, in their stupidity, the South African government wanted nothing to do with them.

I would address these issues later in my life but, as an eager 23-year-old, my mind was full of playing Test cricket and I can hardly describe the sense of excitement and anticipation that preceded South Africa's tour to Australia and New Zealand in the southern hemisphere summer of 1963/64. After two years of nothing, we were going to play five Tests in Australia followed by another three in New Zealand.

Needless to say, I was delighted to be named in the tour group. It was going to be my first visit to that part of the world, and only my second-ever trip abroad. It was not long before that South African touring squads had set sail by boat, so the prospect of jumping aboard a plane was still a novelty.

We flew in a Lockheed Electra, but the plane didn't have the range to reach Perth without refuelling a couple of times, so it was necessary to make a stop in Mauritius. We stayed overnight at a place called Curepipe, a name that originated from the days when sailors would go there to cure their pipes. The place was full of South African expatriates, who entertained us extremely well.

The next stop in our hop, skip and jump across the Indian Ocean was the Cocos Islands, where we landed on a strip of concrete in the middle of the big blue sea. The sand was a dazzling white and the breakers rolled in on either side of the runway. I remember the pilot informing us that we had reached the point of no return. In other words, if anything went wrong with the plane, we would have to carry on rather than turn back because we were closer to Australia than home. My heart was pounding. It was an exciting moment.

We eventually landed in Perth and discovered the famous black swans swimming on the ponds outside the arrivals hall. My first impression was that, in terms of the geography and climate, Perth was a first cousin to Cape Town, and most of us immediately felt pretty much at home.

One evening early in the tour we were invited to watch 'the trots'. I was nonplussed because, in my limited experience, the trots was a bug you didn't want on foreign travel, but it was explained that this was a horse race with a twist. Known as sulky racing in America, it involves a jockey sitting on a miniscule cart harnessed behind the horse, and then hurtling around the racetrack at amazing speeds.

We went along and enjoyed the spectacle. It looked quite danger-ous and several times, as the horses broke into a gallop, one of these light and fragile carts disintegrated after coming away from the har-ness. Even so, the horses looked magnificent, and their high stepping was beautiful.

Some of my teammates enjoyed themselves by having a bet or two on the races, but I resisted the temptation. Not long before, I had met a trainer in a Port Elizabeth pub who had persuaded me to put a reason-able amount of money on a couple of his 'sure things' that were running later that afternoon. I still remember the names of the two horses, Hul-labaloo and Ticha.

At any rate, I was easily persuaded and watched with growing excite-ment as Hullabaloo took the lead. I can still hear the voice of the an-nouncer as the race entered the final straight: "It's Hullabaloo in the lead, Hullabaloo is way ahead, Hullabaloo is 50 yards from the finish... Hullabaloo is down, he won't finish."

Undaunted, and encouraged to recover my losses by my new friend, the trainer, I put more money on this horse called Ticha to win the next race. Initially, she seemed an absolute certainty to win as she ran clear of the field. The announcer continued: "Ticha looks so strong. Oh no, Ticha is down."

That was that. I went home with an empty wallet, resolving never to get involved in betting on horses again; and, after that afternoon in Perth, my resolution remained intact.

Another evening in Perth, we were taken to the studios of the Channel 7 television station, where we met the one and only Diana Dors, one of the most popular actresses at the time. I will not say the South African cricketers were all straining to look down the front of her dress, but only because it was not necessary to strain. Her celebrated pair of assets was perfectly displayed for all to admire.

On the field, it was the performances of a 19-year-old South African batsman which were starting to get the attention of the cricketing world. When Graeme Pollock announced his arrival by scoring an outstanding 125 in 80 minutes against an Australian XI in Perth, people began to take notice. Aside from being amazingly talented, Graeme was tall at 6'3" and looked much older than his age. He also used an extraordinarily heavy bat. While we, the mere mortals, were playing with bats weighing between 2lbs 5oz and 2lbs 8oz, Graeme was hammering away with a three-and-a-half pounder.

The first Test was played at the Woolloongabba ground in Brisbane, known as the Gabba, and the match stands out in my memory for the personal disaster that befell one of the Australian players.

The home team won the toss, batted first and scored 435. Trevor Goddard and I opened our innings in reply, and a likeable Australian fast bowler named Ian Meckiff took the ball to bowl the second over. There had been some muttering that Meckiff had an illegal action and was another 'chucker' who got away with it, something like the New Zealander, Gary Bartlett, whom we had faced two years before.

Well, we didn't think the umpires would be too bothered, until, with Trevor Goddard on strike, Meckiff sent down the second ball of his over and umpire Col Eager called 'No ball'. I was standing at the non-striker's end, and I remember the look of horror on Meckiff's face as he turned to look at the umpire.

It got worse. He was called on the third ball, the fifth ball and the ninth ball. Nobody was laughing by then. It was appalling, and people were starting to wonder if the over would ever end. It did, but Richie Benaud, the Australian captain, had no option but to take him out of the attack.

I found myself standing beside 'Mecko' during the next break, and I saw tears streaming down his cheeks. I sensed players on both sides were affected by what happened. We all felt a great deal of sympathy for this fine cricketer and thoroughly decent man, whose life and cricket career had suddenly been turned upside down. Sad to say, Ian Meckiff never played first class cricket again.

'Mecko' had become another in the line of bowlers branded as chuckers. It's unfortunate, and it's terrible for the player and his family. I always get extremely angry when these fellows are called 'cheats'. I have known quite a few of them, and there is never any element of intent. Without exception, they were decent people, who had either suffered arm defects since birth or been affected by some kind of accident.

Every country has experienced similar situations. There was a South African bowler called Geoff Griffin, whom I first saw playing at the Nuffield Week. People reckoned he had a suspect action in those days, but nothing was said until he had risen through the ranks and was playing for South Africa against England in a Test match, and it was there, of all places, that an umpire finally questioned his action and called 'no ball'.

I can't help thinking Meckiff, Griffin and many others would have been spared a harrowing experience if an umpire at a lower level of the game had had the courage to call him, and so give him the opportunity to resolve the problem. This is generally what happens nowadays but, back then, nobody seemed to worry at club level and these ticking time bombs too often exploded at the highest level of the game.

The Test match in Brisbane was peppered with unusual incidents. Walking out to the middle on the second morning, I noticed several bullets lying on the grass next to the wicket. I drew this to the attention of one of the umpires, a wonderful man called Lou Rowan, who could offer no explanation.

One of the Australians, Wally Grout, saw the funny side of the situation, and walked up to the umpire with a completely straight face, asking: "Could you stand a little bit to the left, Lou, because I can see a man sitting in the stands who is pointing a gun at you and if he misses, I think he could possibly hit me."

We never did solve the mystery of the bullets, although the most likely explanation seemed to be that they had been dropped by one of the night security guards.

Wally was a great character. One evening during that Brisbane test, Peter Carlstein and I spent some time sitting in the changing room and discussing the origins of our surnames. 'Carly', as everyone called him, said he was related to King Carl Gustav of Sweden, and he related how Carl had married a princess from a place called Stein, and their union has created the surname Carlstein.

Not to be outdone, I claimed one of my ancestors had been an alcoholic who was always in pubs and bars, and that when he married into a family called Low, he began calling himself Barlow.

As players, we often received telegrams from back home wishing us luck or whatever, and the next morning we sent Carly one with the message: "Good luck, Gus."

"Who the hell is Gus?" he said, as he read it.

"It must be King Carl Gustav," I replied amid much laughter

Well, Wally Grout somehow heard about our discussion and, when Carly walked out to bat the following day, the Australian welcomed him to the middle with an exaggerated full bow from the hip, and declared: "A very good morning to you, Your Royal Highness". Carly and the Australians burst into fits of laughter.

A few weeks later, when we had moved on to New Zealand, a terrible shadow was cast over our tour by the desperate news that Carly's wife and three children had all been killed in a car accident. The entire squad was stunned, and the tragedy put everything into perspective. We knew the cricket was important, but it wasn't that important, and we did whatever we could to support our teammate.

The third day was washed out by rain, and the Brisbane Test eventually ended as a draw. I was content with my efforts in the first innings, when I managed to score 114, my first century in Test cricket, but I followed that with a humbling duck in the second dig. That is the beauty of the game: just when you think it's easy, and you've just about got everything under control, it knocks you off your perch.

We were all enjoying the tour, not least because of the local girls who always seemed to be hovering around the grounds and our hotels. We were riveted by the picture hats they all seemed to wear, which were the fashion at the time, and we were stunned by the scantiness of their clothing.

It was amazing to us, because we came from a country where any excess was frowned upon and deemed a sin by the Church. South Africa in the 1960s was an ultra-conservative society, and we were astonished to hear the bawdy comments the Australian guys made when these girls walked past in all their finery.

The girls didn't seem at all bothered, laughing and waving at the guys, and happily going on their way. Back home, anyone who said that kind of thing to a girl could expect a 'flattie' across the cheek, or worse.

The Australians were extremely hospitable and there was always plenty to do on the days when we were off, and in the evenings. One night, when we were staying for a few days in the town of Newcastle, New South Wales, we were invited to a concert featuring Joan Sutherland, the Australian diva. The prospect of a night at the opera didn't really appeal to us but, after a while, we decided we might as well go along.

Well, to a man, we were enraptured by the beauty and power of the lady's voice. It was astonishing, and I particularly enjoyed the song called Vilia, from Act II of the Merry Widow by Franz Lehar. More than 30 years later, when I found myself lying in a Singapore hospital bed after suffering a stroke, I asked my wife Cally to go out and buy any CD by Joan Sutherland. She found one and, sure enough, Vilia was there among the tracks. All the happy memories of an exhilarating tour flooded back, and raised my flagging spirits.

Wherever we were in Australia, there was almost always an invitation for us to go somewhere, perhaps to have drinks at the local Yacht

Club, which always seemed a popular destination, or maybe to party at a nightclub where we enthusiastically joined in a fashionable dance called the Stomp.

The tour schedule placed us in Tasmania during Christmas week, 1964, playing a match against the State team in Launceston between the twentieth and the twenty-third, followed by a day of travel on Christmas Eve, a day off on the day itself and a match against a Combined Tasmania team in Hobart from the twenty-sixth until the twenty-eighth. It would be fair to report that few of our squad have endured such a miserable Christmas, before or since.

First, our airplane was delayed on Christmas Eve, which meant we spent most of the day sitting around the departures lounge at Launceston airport, feeling dejected, missing our families and friends back home. Christmas Day was no better, and we 'celebrated' by watching television at the hotel.

I couldn't help thinking that, if the roles had been reversed, and the Australian cricketers had been touring in South Africa over the festive period, we would have welcomed them all into our homes and treated them to a typical South African Christmas. Well, sadly, our hosts were nowhere to be seen.

My mother saved the day. She had kindly dispatched over to Australia a little wooden crate full of goodies, which included a large traditional Christmas cake full of brandy and fruit. I shared it with the whole group after we had suffered a cold and fatty lunch at the hotel, and everyone loved it. Mrs Barlow was hailed as a heroine, and even mentioned in several of Charles Fortune's match commentaries on SABC radio.

We eventually travelled on to Melbourne to play the second Test in the first week of 1964, where we were encouraged to hear that the Australians would have to play without Richie Benaud and several other key players who were injured or sick. Bobby Simpson had been named as the stand-in captain.

I was getting myself ready in the visitors' dressing room at the Melbourne Cricket Ground when Peter Pollock walked past and, all of a sudden, plucked a hair out of my chest.

"What was that for?" I asked, a little irritated by the momentary pain.
"Luck," he smiled.

Well, it worked. I somehow managed to withstand the onslaught of the Australian bowlers and, with wickets falling all around me, eke out a score of 109. Even so, I was not popular. Goddard and Carlstein had both been run out, and it was generally reckoned by my teammates that I had been to blame for both incidents. A message was sent out to me in the middle, saying: "Don't bother to come in for lunch".

The Melbourne Test was drawn but, from that point onwards, the series became a platform for the sustained emergence of one of the very greatest batsmen ever to have played the game, and it was my great privilege to be standing at the opposite end for much of the time, marvelling at R.G. Pollock.

In the third Test in Sydney, we were struggling at 70 for two when Graeme walked out to the crease with that long stride that would become so familiar. He took guard, looked around at the field and thumped the first ball he received over extra cover for a one-bounce four. As one of the senior players in the side, I watched this with alarm and, at the next interval, made a point of offering some advice.

"Hey," I said. "Just take it easy. We're in trouble here. Have a look at the bowling. Calm down."

"Don't worry," Graeme replied, with an impish and disarming grin. "The ball pitched in just the right place."

It became one of the catchphrases of the tour, young Graeme explaining how 'the ball pitched in just the right place', so he just hit it. He proceeded to score a brilliant century but, challenged to chase 409 in the fourth innings, we were left short on 326 for five. The draw meant we still trailed 1-0.

Graeme's nickname on tour was 'Little Dog', because his elder brother Peter was known as 'Pooch'. In the fourth Test at Adelaide, once Australia had scored 345 in the first innings, we were wobbling at 58 for two. Just before tea on the second day, our Little Dog started his innings. He seemed to struggle at first, playing and missing, and to be honest, he was fortunate to survive until the break.

It was a different story in the last session of the day. I was standing at the non-striker's end when the Australian bowler Neil Hawke raced in to bowl. Graeme smashed his first three deliveries for three consecutive boundaries past extra cover, rattling into the picket fence. I had never seen anything like it. With power, grace and perfect timing, he made the business of batting look amazingly simple.

There was no need to hurry down the wicket to tell him to calm down. By now, I had realised that this young genius was playing a different game to the rest of us. If the ball pitched in the right place, as he so liked to say, he would hit it. All we had to do was watch and enjoy the spectacle.

South Africa's total raced beyond 250 by the close of play, and Graeme was in command. We continued our partnership for the fourth wicket the following morning, taking the attack to the Australians and scoring freely. In fact, more than anything, we were really enjoying ourselves, having fun.

I made 201, which eventually proved to be the highest score of my Test career, but Graeme correctly took the praise for his brilliant innings of 175. It was a masterpiece. I was simply the jackal picking at the corpse, after the lion had eaten his fill.

We sensed an opportunity to win, but we needed to bowl out Australia a second time. Their batsmen were hanging around and, at one stage, out in the field, I started badgering Trevor Goddard to give me the ball, and let me bowl. I'm not sure the captain enjoyed my antics. He looked irritated, but I persisted.

Such behaviour would become a feature of my cricket career: we would be struggling for a breakthrough, and I would get an idea in my head that I would be able to get the essential wicket. I'm afraid it was never in my nature to keep quiet, so I would start pestering the captain.

People thought I was cocky, but I wasn't. It all boiled down to this: I reckoned I was lucky.

When I was at school, I could clearly remember a history lesson where we were taught how Napoleon had told his generals that, above all, they must be lucky, and that quote stuck in my mind. As much as anything,

I wanted to make sure I was a lucky cricketer. How? By working hard. Gary Player, the great South African golfer, famously said: 'The more I practise, the luckier I get.' I took that to heart as well.

So I did work hard, and I did think I was lucky; and, at times, not always, but quite often, I used to get a feeling that I could do the trick. With hindsight, it was all to do with the power of positive thinking.

In years to come, some knowledgeable observers, such as the respected cricket writer Louis Duffus, made some kind remarks to the effect that, during the 1960s, my approach had helped the South African cricket team take a more positive approach to Test cricket, going out to 'get on the front foot' and dominate matches, rather than just sit back and be conservative and, in a sense, limit the damage.

Well, if this was the case, other players certainly played their part. Touring Australia in 1963/4, we were a young team, bordering on brash. With cricketers like Graeme in our ranks, we didn't stand back for any-body, and we thought we were capable of winning the series.

At any rate, we needed a wicket in Adelaide. Trevor eventually got fed up with me asking to bowl, and he handed me the ball. I dismissed Shep-herd in my first over, Richie Benaud in my third and Garth McKenzie not long afterwards. My 'luck' held, and we won the Test by ten wickets, squaring the series.

We had enjoyed our week in Adelaide, not least because, during the Test, we had the opportunity to spend some time with perhaps the city's most famous citizen.

Don Bradman was one of the Australian selectors at the time, and he watched the entire match. At the end of the third day's play, a group of us had joined him for a drink. 'The Don' was naturally impressed with the way Graeme had taken the game to the bowlers, and I can clearly recall him telling the youngster: "If you're going to bat like that again, let me know, and I'll come and watch."

He had a tremendous presence and, as he discussed cricket, he gave me the impression of being far ahead of the way most of us were approaching the game. He was an original thinker who seemed to see everything so clearly and whose soft-spoken opinions made perfect sense. When we left him later that evening, I felt a genuine sense of disappointment that I would never have the chance to be a member of his team.

With the series level at 1-1 and one Test still to play, there should have been an overwhelming sense of excitement and purpose within our squad, but it wasn't like that. In my view – and this is only my view because, within any touring group, as in any group, there is always a wide range of perspectives – as we continued the tour, there was a distinctly unpleasant atmosphere within our squad.

It seemed to me there were two reasons:

First, just before the fourth Test, there had been an unfortunate incident involving Johnny Waite and Denis Lindsay. As I recall, Johnny had not been feeling well but he went to the races on the evening before the game and it was assumed he would be OK to play. However, he arrived at the Adelaide Oval on the morning of the first day and announced he was not fit to play. Everybody was a little surprised, but the main consequence of his unavailability was that someone else would have to keep wicket.

Denis had arrived at the ground some time before, and had already made his way down the nets where he had started his practice routine. He was the kind of cricketer who liked to be fully prepared and, when he was informed at such short notice that he would have to take the gloves, he was annoyed. A row followed, with some harsh words being spoken on both sides. The mood in the team had soured.

Second, again in my view, the approach of the team management, who insisted on treating us like a bunch of naughty schoolboys, did not help the general spirit of the side.

After the Test in Adelaide, I had naturally gone out to celebrate our win. But, before leaving the hotel, trying to be well organised, I packed everything into my suitcase, and carefully left out the shirt, tie, trousers and blazer that I would have to wear when we flew to Sydney the next day. That was my intention.

Unfortunately, later that evening, while I was out, the team bus driver decided to go around all the players' rooms, collecting the suitcases and taking them down to the bus. He wanted to make a smooth start the next day, and get to the airport early. When he came to my room, he saw the pile of clothes and, thinking he was doing me a favour, packed them in my suitcase, which he proceeded to put in the bus.

I arrived back to the hotel later that night, saw what had happened and realised there was no option but to travel in the clothes I was wearing. The misunderstanding was not my fault.

Ken Viljoen, our tour manager, known as 'Boss', unfortunately did not share my view. I tried to explain what had happened, but he said he was not interested in excuses.

"I made it very clear that anybody wearing the wrong gear would be sent home on a slow boat," he said, echoing the words of a popular song, which became his favourite phase.

I was not in the mood to submit. Adamant that I had not done anything wrong, and angry that I was being blamed, I replied: "You don't have to worry, Boss, I'll pay my own fare."

The argument escalated, and Trevor Goddard had to step in to calm things down.

Boss imposed a strict curfew on us, ruling that we had to be back in our hotels by ten o'clock every night, and we generally observed the regulation. We were a young team, and he probably thought it was necessary from him to be cruel to be kind, but we didn't always see it that way.

On one occasion, we went to the cinema and the film ran longer than we expected, meaning we were going to arrive back after the curfew. As we approached the hotel, we asked the taxi driver to turn the engine off and quietly freewheel down the hill before coming to a halt at the main entrance. This charade was necessary because we were desperate not to be caught by the Boss, who was usually waiting for us.

We got away with being late on that occasion, but some of the Australian players heard about the incident, and mocked us for being so meek. They said they would just have ignored the curfew.

The other complaint about the manager was his negative attitude. He always seemed to be finding fault with our performance. We would arrive back in the pavilion after a tough session in the field and he would typically say something like, 'Well done, but it's a pity about that dropped catch'.

Even then, as a 23-year old, I remember saying to myself that if I ever found myself in a similar position, presiding over a cricket team, I would always try to be positive. I'm sure I didn't always succeed, but it's simply the case that positive attitudes in the dressing room yield positive results on the field.

So, a combination of the simmering row between Waite and Lindsay and the team management's general approach meant the mood within our squad was not what it should have been.

A team meeting was called to discuss the problems, and most of us felt the open, frank discussion helped put the tour back on track. Some conflict is inevitable on sports tours. When a relatively small group of necessarily strong and forthright characters spends so much time in such close proximity, under pressure to perform, small issues can quickly spiral into seething arguments. It is the responsibility of the management and captain to keep things in perspective and, by holding the meeting, eventually that was done.

So we arrived in Sydney, knowing that victory in the fifth Test would give us a rare series win over Australia, in Australia, and surprise the cricket world. We didn't doubt we had the talent, and the momentum to win, but, in the end, our relative youth meant we lacked the experience to complete the job.

We started the Test well, dismissing Australia for 311 and then building a 100-run lead on the first innings. Bowling them out again for just 270, we were left requiring just 171 to win the series. But there was not enough time, and we were finally left stranded on 76 for no wicket.

The match, and the series, was drawn.

Some people subsequently criticised us for missing an excellent opportunity to win and, to be honest, there was a sense of mild disappointment in our dressing room after the match, but we remained a young South African team, and our performance suggested the future was bright.

Personally I had enjoyed Australia, and I seriously considered living there for a while. The weather is great, and the bold, upbeat approach to life would have suited me down to the ground. Unfortunately it never happened, but there will always be a soft place in my heart for Australians and their country.

The only souvenir from the 1963/64 tour I kept was a small silver boomerang, decorated with an Australian opal in the centre. These beautiful little things were presented to each of the South African players by the Governor of New South Wales at a cocktail party in Sydney. We were all thrilled, not least because the gift made such a welcome change from the usual exchange of ties.

I must have had more than 300 cricket ties in my possession and when my wife Cally asked me what they all were and where they came from, I could put a name to only about half of them. The unknown ones were given to the farm staff who used them to keep their trousers up, among other things.

By the end of February 1964, we had been away for almost four months but nobody was thinking of going home because we still had three Tests to play in New Zealand.

The atmosphere in the Land of the Long White Cloud was completely different from Australia. For a start, the weather seemed to be much colder and the cricket facilities were extremely poor, to say the least. Only Eden Park in Auckland, could really have been described as a proper ground, and that was primarily a rugby stadium. The quality of the practice pitches everywhere made training almost impossible.

Most New Zealanders didn't seem particularly interested in cricket and the only time they really got excited was when they asked us about the state of South African rugby. The Springboks were due to tour New Zealand in 1965, and everybody wanted to know if we thought they would beat the All Blacks.

The first Test was played at a ground called the Basin Reserve in Wellington. Well, there were enough holes around the place to resemble several basins. The place was in a shocking state, and there is no doubt that, judged by today's standards, the ground would have been declared unfit for Test cricket. In our day, we just had a look at the wicket, maybe had a bit of a grumble and got on with the game.

With the boys on tour... from left, Tony Pithey, Joe Partridge, Kelly Seymour and me

A quiet moment on tour, reading a letter from Mum

Pops and Mum, my two greatest supporters, posed for this picture, listening to radio commentary of our Test matches in Australia, 1964

A group of Springboks with Diana Dors in Australia, 1964… trying not to look down her dress

Trevor Goddard, right, leads South Africa onto the field during the Test in Melbourne, 1964

In Adelaide, I spent some time with two of the greatest batsmen of all time, the young Graeme Pollock and the unique Don Bradman

It was a privilege for me to bat alongside Graeme Pollock in the Adelaide Test, 1964, and here we look quite pleased with our record partnership

I remember the weather was bitterly cold, and the pace of the match was funereal. Just over 300 runs were scored on the first two days, and a result never looked likely. John Reid was still captaining the New Zealand team and, with memories of the tempestuous 61/62 series in South Africa still in our minds, we were expecting him to produce a new barrage of bumpers, or words. Maybe it was just too cold.

We travelled on to play the second Test in Dunedin, where our understanding of the phrase 'Test cricket' took on a new dimension. This Test had very little to do with cricket, and everything to do with a 'test' of surviving in temperatures that can only be described as arctic. I had never seen so many jumpers being worn on a cricket field, with most of us wearing two in our efforts to withstand the biting wind.

Once again, both teams struggled to take many wickets and, in front of very few brave souls in the stands, the Test petered out into that draw that had always seemed probable.

Happily, a pale sun appeared over the horizon during the third Test at Eden Park, which meant we were able to enjoy the relatively balmy experience of a 'one-jersey' game. Batting first, Trevor Goddard and I put together a reasonable opening stand, and Colin Bland scored a wonderful 83. Our total of 371 put the home team under a bit of pressure and, when we bowled them out for 263, we sensed an opportunity.

Trevor called for some quick runs in our second innings, and he eventually made a very sporting declaration at 200 for five. We had a come a long way to play this series, and we were eager to force a positive result, rather than just kill the game and return home on the back of three dull draws.

All we had to do was bowl them out, and we tried. Our bowlers put the ball in the right place, but a series of excellent appeals were turned down, and the match was drawn. Tempers flared on the final day of the match, and most of us developed sore throats from our increasingly loud appealing, but to no avail. Sadly, the quality of the umpiring in New Zealand did not match the excellent standard in South Africa.

The three-Test series in New Zealand may not have been notable for the cricket, but it did provide us with a first glimpse of the anti-apartheid demonstrations that would dog South African sports teams from the mid-1960s onwards. None of us properly appreciated the issues at the time, and we regarded the various acts of disruption and shouting as not much more than an entertaining diversion.

During one match, a committed group of protesters managed to get into the ground overnight and start digging up what they thought was the pitch. Unfortunately for them, they damaged the wrong strip and our match was unaffected. Mind you, it was an easy error to make. The match pitch was so underprepared and green, it was hard enough to identify in broad daylight, let alone in the middle of the night.

After the third and final Test, some of the South African players decided to spend a few more days in New Zealand, seeing the sights, but I was among the group that headed straight home. The 22-week trip had been an unforgettable experience, but I was eager to see my family and friends again.

Chapter Six – Test Days (1964-67)

Every MCC tour to South Africa is eagerly awaited, but the visit of Ted Dexter's England team in the summer of 1964/65 generated exceptional excitement among the players and public because South Africans reckoned we had a decent chance of winning.

We had shown promise the previous year in Australia and New Zealand, and the Australians had never tired of telling us how we were going to beat the Poms. I suppose we started to believe them, and maybe succumbed to a little complacency.

When the England team toured overseas in those days, they did so under the name of the Marylebone Cricket Club, and, from a South African perspective, it was the plum series. The links between the two countries ran deep and most of our players had spent some time playing either club or county cricket in England.

Then, as now, it was regularly said that world cricket needs a strong England team, and, whatever their form, they were always a respected, important and highly regarded touring squad.

South African cricket supporters were particularly looking forward to seeing Ted Dexter in action. The elegant, fluent batsman was hailed as the game's next superstar, but there were other players who occupied our thoughts, like the bustling Ken Barrington and a bespectacled young opener called Geoffrey Boycott.

'Boycs' certainly knew how to occupy his crease, make no mistake, and there were many occasions when his determination hauled England out of trouble. His style of play wasn't particularly endearing, but the game takes all sorts, and, even then, in his youth, we certainly respected him as an opponent.

The first Test of the five-match series was played at Kingsmead in Durban, and the English batsmen wasted no time in stamping their mark on the contest. They took control by scoring freely, enabling Dexter to declare at 495 for nine. As usual, Trevor Goddard and I opened our reply.

England's opening bowler was Ian Thompson and in his second over he sent down a delivery that I judged to be a full and fast yorker. I quickly brought my bat down to block the ball on the crease, but was surprised to see the ball fly into the hands of second slip. The MCC players appealed loudly and, reckoning there was no way the ball could have travelled so far without hitting some part of my bat, I decided there was no point waiting for the umpire's decision and decided to 'walk', out for 2.

Some doubt persisted in my mind as I made my way to the pavilion, and I began to wonder whether I had not perhaps hit the ball into the ground, from where it bounced to the slip fielder.

Nowadays, a dismissed batsman only has to look at the TV replay in the dressing room to see if he was out, but, back in those days, before the advent of television, we had to be a little more patient before we discovered if justice had been done. There was a documentary news film called the African Mirror, which was shown at cinemas every week, and it usually carried some footage from the Test. So I made my way to the movies after the match, and was annoyed when I sat in the cinema and clearly saw I had hit the ball into the ground before the catch.

In any case, we were bowled out for 155, and asked to follow on 340 runs behind. We felt humiliated and unable to turn the tide. I scored another big fat zero in the second innings. So did Graeme Pollock, and South Africa ended up losing the first Test of the series against England by an innings and plenty.

Dexter's team had seemed so calm and confident and they looked like repeating the dose in the second Test at the Wanderers, when they took control by batting first and making a big score. We followed on again, but then dug deep in the second innings and managed to hold out for the draw.

This set the tone for the rest of the series. England were content to play relatively conservative cricket and to protect their 1-0 lead and we struggled to find the inspiration or firepower to bowl them out twice. The result was a cricketing stalemate that delivered less than outstanding entertainment for the spectators. I was as frustrated as anybody by the dull pace, but the series was not without controversy.

The third Test at Newlands seemed to be drifting towards another draw, and I was batting, facing the gentle spin bowling of Fred Titmus. Wanting to be positive, I tried to use my feet and get down the wicket, but I didn't get the timing right. The ball hit me on the toe and my bat clattered against my instep. The ball looped up to slip, and the England fielders started shouting: "Catch it, catch it, catch it."

I was certain the ball had come off my foot, not my bat, so I stood my ground.

"Well caught, well caught, well caught," they all shouted, turning to umpire expecting him, pressurising him to send me on my way. Well, he didn't, and I could sense the fielders were irritated.

I took a single off the next ball and, as I reached the non-striker's end, I unmistakably heard Titmus say the word 'cheat' in my direction. That was enough. The ball had hit my foot. In fact, my foot was bloody sore from the blow, and this guy was calling me a cheat. I wanted to knock his block off, and, with my bat in the air, I advanced towards him. I was angry. He looked petrified and scuttled away to the covers. The thought did occur to me that I should chase him but common sense prevailed and I returned to the crease.

The incident created a bad atmosphere between the teams, and in fact some of the England players made a point of not clapping when I eventually reached three figures. The matter didn't rest there. Soon after England began their innings. Ken Barrington went to cut a ball from Peter Pollock. We all heard a definite snick, but he just stood there. The umpire decided he was 'not out', and then Barrington walked.

Everybody was mindful of the flare-up between Titmus and me, and Barrington's behaviour was variously interpreted as an attempt to make the umpire appear stupid for giving him not out or a way of showing me up for not 'walking'. Either way, it didn't go down well with us. Some of the English players reckoned Ken had given me a lesson in 'walking', but the difference was that he was out, and I wasn't.

At the end of the day's play, Titmus came to our changing room and, looking at me, said: "I have been told to apologise to you". That was inadequate. The apology should have come directly from him, not because he had been told to say sorry by his captain, MJK Smith. He didn't seem remotely contrite and I'm afraid I responded by telling him to go forth and multiply, in rather more blunt and economical language.

Of course, the animosity didn't last and, in fact, Fred and I always have a laugh about it whenever we meet, but it certainly soured relations between the teams during the 1964/65 series.

The issue of 'to walk or not to walk' has always aroused strong feelings among cricketers. Some reckon that if you know you have hit the ball and you are out, then you should do the honourable thing and walk. Others feel it is the umpire's job to decide whether you are out or not out, and you should leave it to him and get on with the game. They say that, over the season, the good decisions will even out the bad.

Today, the latter view is generally held and hardly anybody walks any more. When I was playing, most of the England batsmen did choose to walk. Or so they said. There was one prominent, celebrated England batsman who always walked if England were doing well but, if his team happened to be in trouble and the chips were down, he would stand and survive by virtue of his noble reputation as a 'walker'.

"Oh," the umpire would think, as the fielding side erupted in a universal appeal for a clear nick. "He usually walks, and he's standing his ground, so he can't possibly have touched it."

Thus the batsman would survive. It happened more than once, and again and again players would get upset, and teams would fall out. On thing is certain: the 'walking' dilemma will run and run.

The fourth Test was played at the Wanderers and we produced a stronger performance. I managed to score 96 before being caught and bowled, and for some time it seemed as if we might be able to force a victory and so draw level in the series, but we were frustrated by the deeply determined Boycott, who dropped anchor at the crease and saw England through difficult moments and safely home to yet another draw.

Still 1-0 down, our need was therefore desperate in the fifth and final Test at St George's Park, but we and the Port Elizabeth crowd alike suffered more frustration. England had evidently decided to play themselves into an unassailable position before taking any risks and making any effort to win the match. Any suggestion that they had an obligation to entertain the crowd would have been dismissed as nonsense.

We tried. Having scored 502 in the first innings, our attempts to bowl them out and force the follow-on were thwarted by the familiar barriers of Boycott and Barrington. Goddard asked for quick runs in our second innings, and he declared at lunch on the fifth day, setting England a sporting 246 to win. The challenge was declined, time ebbed away and, with rain about, the Test meandered its way to another draw.

It had been a miserable series. There is no doubt we played the more aggressive cricket, but the absence of several key players through injury had deprived us of a cutting edge.

Needless to say, the hierarchy of South African cricket sought a scapegoat for the disappointment of a series defeat, and they settled on the blameless Goddard as the man to carry the can. The national selectors shamefully asked him to resign as captain on the grounds that the responsibility was affecting his batting. It seemed as if they didn't even have the guts to sack him, and Trevor rightly refused the request.

This was no way to treat a very decent man who had given his all for his country and shown great skill in nurturing a young team. Maybe it was this sequence of events that persuaded Trevor to make himself unavailable for the tour to England later that year. That was my impression but, wherever the truth lies, there is no question we missed his presence and leadership. I also missed him as my opening partner.

Peter van der Merwe was named captain of the South African team to tour England in 1965, to the surprise of many in the media, who proceeded to give him a rough ride. We had anticipated that Johnny Waite, the Transvaal captain, would automatically take over from Trevor and that would be that, but the selectors appeared to have decided that Peter, a former Bishops boy who had become captain of Western Province, had the right pedigree for the job, and he got the nod.

Some of the journalists never really accepted him, which was unfortunate, but Peter's attitude won over the players and, with Jack Plimsoll making a big contribution as a quiet and effective manager, we developed into a contented, positive team prepared to work hard and earn success.

Our trip to England proved an adventure in itself, as our plane stopped to refuel at Leopoldville in what was then known as the Belgian Congo, and then again at Nairobi, in Kenya. Our third and last stop was Athens, and I was allowed to sit in the cockpit beside the pilot for take-off from the Greek capital.

"This runway is not up to international standards," the pilot told me, casually, as he flicked switches and the plane began to gather speed before lifting itself majestically into the air.

"Oh, really," I said, trying to appear unconcerned.

There was an olive grove at the end of the runway and, for a terrible moment, I thought we were going to clip the tops of the trees as we passed above. We didn't, and were soon flying above the deep blue Mediterranean Sea. Some months later, however, that is exactly what happened to a plane carrying some friends of ours back to South Africa and, so I was told, the undercarriage was severely damaged.

At any rate, we arrived in the middle of the English summer, and found ourselves in similar temperatures to those we had left behind in the South African winter. The only difference was that it was raining in England. As we would soon discover, our entire tour was destined to be plagued by bad weather.

The first match against Derbyshire was played in drizzle and an icy wind, and we not only lost the game but also didn't get any chance to practise. Chelmsford was our next destination, for a match against Essex, where we played better, but the match was notable for a group of anti-apartheid demonstrators who were making their way to the ground, but suffered the indignity of falling into a river when a small bridge collapsed.

Needless to say, the South Africans were highly amused by this spectacle and, most of the time, we did take a fairly light-hearted approach to the protesters. Many hours were spent watching the group, working out which was the prettiest woman among them, and deciding who would invite her to dinner, and perhaps get some inside information about what the demos were planning.

There were also times when some of the guys actually read the ban-

ners with slogans demanding the end of apartheid and freedom for political prisoners, and I would watch them deep in thought. In fact, now
and then the demonstrations provoked some interesting debate on the
team bus.

I usually participated in these discussions, but, for the most part, we
were young cricketers who didn't worry too much about what was regarded as the politics of the day. We had travelled to England to play
cricket, hopefully to win the series, and that is where we focused our
attention.

The first Test at Lord's was significant as the hundredth match between
England and South Africa, and I can still recall the fantastic atmosphere
of excitement and expectation on the first morning. As a schoolboy it had
always been my greatest dream to walk through the Grace gates, make
my way to the pavilion, reach the changing room and gaze at the boards
listing all the players who had either scored Test centuries or taken five
wickets in a Test innings at the ground, and then to walk out and represent my country.

In 1965 this dream came true for me. There are many small traditions
and regulations that make Lord's so special, and it is these quirks that
give the place depth and history. It saddens me when I hear modern players complaining about Lord's and its ways, making disparaging remarks
about fuddy-duddies and particular rules that they don't understand.
The fact is Lord's will be standing long after those guys are forgotten.

Back in 1965, we stayed that week at the Waldorf Hotel, on the Ald-
wych in the West End of London, which seemed very grand to a bunch
of colonials like us, but the Test was peppered by a series of little niggles
reflecting the poor atmosphere between the teams, lingering from the
64/65 series.

England batted first, and Peter Pollock bowled with real intent. It
wasn't long before he got involved in some verbal sparring with David
Brown, but we were astonished when the England batsman wandered
over and actually pushed Peter in the middle of his run-up. I had never
seen anything like it. Peter continued to race in, and one of his quicker
deliveries hit the head of John Edrich, who fell down and retired hurt.

We were not standing back, and I was pleased. It seemed to us that, for many years, South Africa has been regarded as a soft touch in international cricket but, through the 1960s, in successive series against New Zealand, Australia and now against England, this Springbok team had shown we would give as good as we got out there in the middle. We played hard and fair, but we would be nobody's pushovers.

Once again, we reckoned England played conservative cricket and a draw always seemed likely, but the Test was graced by the superb performance of Colin Bland. He made 70 in our first innings, and then thrilled the Lord's crowd with the athleticism of his fielding. At one point he swooped on the ball at deep square leg and ran out Ken Barrington with a direct hit, collecting and throwing the ball in one fluent movement.

The Fleet Street press swiftly christened him the 'Golden Eagle', and reported that Blandy had confirmed his reputation as the outstanding fielder in the world. I agreed with them. He was a great natural athlete, but he also spent hours practising what he regarded as the art of fielding.

I once heard that, when he was a prefect at Milnerton College, his enthusiasm for fielding led to the creation of a novel punishment for naughty boys. Whenever he wanted to practise, an offending pupil would be ordered to take the wicket-keeping gloves, and catch the ball, which Blandy threw in, over and over again, from various parts of the field. After a while, the boy's hands would look like plates of liver.

For the second Test we headed to Trent Bridge, where the Pollock brothers came to the fore and inspired one of the most celebrated victories in the history of South African cricket.

Graeme started the show. Our first five wickets went down like skittles, but he marched in and stroked 125 runs from 145 balls in two and a half hours of sheer brilliance. He blasted no fewer than 21 boundaries, but this was not a slog. It was a masterpiece of dominating, classic stroke play. The last 91 of his runs were scored off just 90 balls in 70 minutes, while his partner, Peter van der Merwe, scored 10. This book is not packed with statistics, but these numbers go some way to telling the tale of one of the greatest innings that I have ever seen, played in the context of an intensely competitive Test match on an awkward pitch.

We were ultimately dismissed for 269, and we really needed a quick breakthrough before stumps on the first day. It was brother Peter who duly obliged, removing Boycott for 0 and Barrington for 1.

In truth, we never looked back and Graeme even weighed in with a wicket, trapping MJK Smith lbw for 24 in the second innings. Our victory by 94 runs was thoroughly deserved, and it was all the sweeter for the arduous, frustrating months we had spent desperately trying to win a Test against England.

On the spur of the moment, perhaps an hour or so after the end of the Test, some of us returned to the middle wearing nothing but our underpants, and proceeded to underline our success by watering the wicket, just as we had 'pissed' on the English during the match. It wasn't classy, but somebody took a photograph, which was published in newspapers back home, and most people loved it.

Peter Pollock finished with match figures of 10 for 87 runs in 48 overs, the best analysis of any South African in England. He had made a 'pact with the Lord' that, if he won, he would give up booze. Well, he did abstain from a celebratory drink, at least until he decided the Lord would be satisfied with two hours of penance, whereupon he happily drank a bottle of beer as if it was nectar. He had earned every last drop.

One-nil up with one to play, our task was not yet done.

The last match of the three-Test series was played back in London at the Kennington Oval and, in truth, we were only saved from defeat by a lucky turn in the weather.

Honours were even after the first innings and, when we scored 392 in the second innings, thanks to a solid century by Blandy, we reckoned the game was safe. In fact, it wasn't because the England team that had played such cautious, frankly dull cricket in so many of our encounters over the past nine months suddenly produced the most dazzling stroke play. We were in trouble, and we deliberately began to slow the game down, taking our time between overs. The crowd was not pleased, and started to boo and whistle, but we didn't mind. England had got up to the same tricks earlier in the season, and it was perfectly legal.

Still, the England batsmen prospered. Barrington made 73 and Colin Cowdrey stroked his way to an elegant 78, reaching a point where they seemed favourites to win, needing 91 runs in 70 minutes.

We needed a rainmaker and, literally out of the blue, one large solitary cloud scudded across an otherwise clear sky, turning blacker and blacker. It was directly above us when we felt the first drops. They felt like manna from heaven, and the consequent downpour washed out the rest of the match. To our great relief, the Test was drawn, and South Africa celebrated only their second ever series win in England.

Victory was sweet, very sweet, and we were able to enjoy our last port of call of the tour, the Scarborough festival on the east coast of England. The cricket was relaxed and fun, although there was one shock in store for me when I hit a straight six that struck a lady directly in the stomach. She was walking through the main gate at the time and was terribly shocked. I was also very upset, but she recovered.

On our return home we were hailed as heroes who had restored pride to South African cricket, and, after four months apart, I was thrilled to be reunited with Helen again. Our son Craig had been born just before we left for England in early June, and I returned to discover a bouncing baby boy of four months. He was christened the following week, with my brother Norman and Peter Pollock as his godfathers, and Elizabeth Schreuder, the wife of Ron, the personnel director at SA Breweries, as his godmother.

It was a happy day. In that era, when travel was a luxury, wives and children never accompanied players on tour, and the prolonged periods apart were often hard for young families to bear.

Being able to spend more time at home was just about the only positive aspect of the fact that the political shackles were starting to close around South African sport. An international boycott gained widespread support as an effective vehicle for the outside world to express its opposition to apartheid.

Fully sixteen inactive months had passed since the downpour at the Oval until 23 December, 1966, when the South African cricket team took the field for the opening Test of a five-match series against the touring Australian team, captained by Bobby Simpson. It took place at the new Wanderers stadium, the scaffolding bowl that would become affectionately known as 'the Bullring'.

Remarkably, our side showed just one change from 1965, with Trevor Goddard returning to the fold in place of Jackie Botten, yet the general expectation was that Australia would prove too strong. I'm not sure of the reason but, over the years, South African cricket supporters have never struck me as the most optimistic breed. Having said that, I suppose it is true that such pessimists are never disappointed.

Graham Mackenzie got stuck into our top order on that first morning, and only a battling sixth wicket stand of 110 between 'Sporty' Lindsay and 'Tiger' Lance enabled us to achieve a degree of respectability. However, our first innings total of 199 was looking inadequate as Bobby Simpson and Bill Lawry eased to 99 without loss by the close of play. There were a few frowns of concern in our changing room that evening.

Things didn't go much better the next morning and, even when we had managed to get rid of the openers, the Australian middle order seemed well set. I started to get that itchy feeling again, and I asked Peter if it might be possible for me to have a bowl. I felt lucky, confident, and asked again.

He agreed and, in under an hour, I had taken three wickets for 39, having Paul Redpath, Bob Cowper and Keith Stackpole all three caught behind by the impeccable Sporty Lindsay. Trevor Goddard and Athol McKinnon chipped in and, when the Australians were all out for 325, Sporty had taken six catches in the innings, equalling what was then the world record. We were suddenly right back in the game.

Our second innings was always going to be a real dogfight, but we knuckled down to the task. I chipped in with 50, but it was Graeme Pollock who swung the match in our favour with another outstanding innings. On this occasion, he scored 90 runs in 114 minutes, producing yet another masterpiece of an innings with the casual air of a man who was spending just another day the office... some day, some office.

Sporty sustained the onslaught, and his epic innings of 182 enabled us to reach a total of 620, then South Africa's highest-ever score in a Test and the third highest second innings in Test history. From a very poor position at stumps on the first day, we had shown real guts and determination to fight back and get to a position where we were able to set the Australians an almost impossible target of 495 to win.

Bob Simpson made a gutsy start to their innings, but Trevor Goddard took the ball and began to mesmerise the touring batsmen. Varying his pace and movement, he took six wickets for 53 runs, and our historic victory was eventually secured by a margin of 233 runs. It was South Africa's first home win over Australia in 22 attempts and 64 years of trying. We lifted Trevor onto our shoulders, and chaired him off the field.

Amid all the celebrations, there was some sadness. Colin Bland had been sprinting after the ball towards the boundary when he collapsed as he bent down to flip it back just inside the fence. Everybody immediately realised his knee had gone, and so it proved. Blandy never played another Test, but the marvellous spirit and commitment he had demonstrated in his chase was reflected through the entire team.

As a group, we were determined to take the contest to our opponents, to get on the front foot, literally and figuratively. More than anything, we wanted the days when South African cricketers felt second-best and usually finished second best to disappear into the history books, and a combination of our team spirit and the four or five genuine world-class players in our ranks enabled us to achieve this goal.

We approached the second Test with confidence, even though it was to be played at Newlands, Cape Town, the ground that many cricketers of my generation reckoned was our jinx venue.

It certainly seemed so as the Australians won the toss, elected to bat and set about compiling the large total required to take command. Bob Simpson led from the front with an excellent 153, and Keith Stackpole seemed to be on his way to a century when, on the last ball before tea on the first day, I bowled him a bouncer. He couldn't resist the hook, and we all heard a clear nick as the ball flew through to Sporty.

"Howzat!" I implored, in the umpire's direction.

Howard Kidson, the umpire, didn't move a muscle.

Stackpole tucked his bat under his arm, and walked towards the pavilion. In his mind, he was just heading back to the pavilion for tea at the end of the afternoon session, but the umpire thought he was 'walking', and promptly raised his finger. The Australian batsman looked round in horror, but it was too late. He was out. He looked aghast, but, so far as we were concerned, justice had been done. The incident raised the temperature of the contest but, despite my five for 85, the best analysis of my Test career, the tourists reached 542.

We were struggling. Both the Pollock brothers and Richard Dumbrill were carrying injuries but, as it turned out, even Graeme with a thigh strain proved more than equal to the occasion.

The young master batted with his usual aplomb and thumped 30 boundaries in yet another extraordinary innings of 209, which was then the highest individual score in a Test match at Newlands. However, he didn't have much support from the rest of us, and we were unable to avoid the follow-on.

Our dressing room was starting to resemble a battlefield. Everyone seemed to be suffering some kind of cut or strain, although Sporty's ailment was the most dramatic and he needed stitches in a head cut. Without alarm, the Australians cantered to a six-wicket victory, levelling the series at 1-1.

I managed to make a bit of unwanted history right at the start of the third Test in Durban by being the first batsman to get out before the Test began. We were put in to bat and, for some reason, play started with the clock at Kingsmead showing three minutes before 11 o'clock. I took guard and hit the very first ball of the Test back into the hands of Graham Mackenzie, to be caught and bowled for nought. As I walked back to the pavilion, I looked up to the clock and saw it was 10.58, still two minutes before play was due to start.

Three more wickets fell in quick succession, but Sporty stuck around and scored an excellent 137, taking our innings to respectability at 300 all out.

Our strategy was to unleash a four-pronged pace attack on the Australians, spearheaded by Peter Pollock, who peppered Bill Lawry with bouncers. One of these deliveries reared up of a good length, and opened a severe cut above Bill's eye, leaving a flap of skin hanging over his eye.

There was blood everywhere, and the Australian opener was carted off to hospital, where he had ten stitches sewn into his forehead. He returned to the ground soon afterwards and, his head swathed in bandages, this brave man resumed his innings, and indeed top-scored with 44.

In this match the Australians were confronted by more than the familiar battery of Pollock, Goddard and yours truly.

A dynamic young fast bowler named Mike Procter was making his Test debut for South Africa, and he worried the Australians with his raw pace and ability to swing the ball. 'Proc' took three for 27 in the first innings, and four for 71 in the second, and we ran out comfortable winners by eight wickets.

We were a self-assured team by now, and we fired on all cylinders in the fourth Test at the Wanderers, with Procter taking another four wickets as the Australians crumbled to 143 all out. Sporty Lindsay was having a great series with the bat and, as he scored another century, 131 in our first innings of 332, he established a new world record for the most runs scored by a wicketkeeper in a Test series.

Procter, Pollock and Goddard set about the tourists again and reduced them to 148 for eight just after tea on the final day, facing an innings defeat, when the heavens opened and the Test was drawn.

Word reached our changing room that the Australians were fighting among themselves, with some of their players backing Bobby Simpson as captain, and others dissenting. It was always going to be tough for Bob to fill the shoes left by Richie Benaud, the previous captain, but he was also unfortunate to face a strong South African team, which had been developing and improving for several seasons.

Peter van der Merwe requested a 'green top' for the fifth and final Test at St George's Park in Port Elizabeth, which the groundsman duly delivered. Our battery of fast bowlers charged in and dismissed the Australians for a total of 137. Graeme then marked his twenty-third birthday in the best way possible, by scoring what was his sixth Test century, against the Australians in front of his home crowd in Port Elizabeth.

The family celebrations continued when Peter trapped Ian Redpath lbw in the second innings, and became the fourth, and youngest, South African to take 100 wickets in Test cricket.

We eventually needed just 176 to win the match and, with three down, Tiger Lance scored the winning runs by pulling a majestic, towering six over the head of mid-wicket and into the crowd.

Nobody had imagined we would beat Australia 3-1, yet that is what happened. South Africa was becoming recognised as one of the strongest, if not the strongest, team in the world. It seemed to many pundits that, after getting bogged down against the English, we had cut loose against the Australians.

Life couldn't get any better, or so we thought.

It could, but first it would get worse.

Chapter Seven – Halcyon Days

The MCC were due to tour South Africa in the 1968/69 season, and we all anticipated that the tour would go ahead as planned. Politics hardly entered our minds. Yes, we knew South Africa had been banned from the Olympic Games, and had also been thrown out of FIFA, the governing body of football, but in our neat, little cocoon, we believed our old friends in rugby and cricket would ensure contact was sustained.

It might seem strange now but, if you had asked any South African player in 1968 whether the England tour would go ahead in 1968/69, he would have replied 'Of course', and wondered why you were asking. A major storm was brewing all around us, but the truth is most of us never saw it coming.

The first sign of trouble was when Colin Bland was refused permission to play in a World XI in England. The news came out of the blue, and we started to wonder what would happen. Still, the message from Lord's could not have been clearer: the England tour to South Africa would go ahead.

Basil D'Oliveira's name was beginning to appear in newspaper headlines. This talented all-rounder from Cape Town had moved north, and was making his mark in the England team that played Australia during the northern hemisphere summer of 1968. When he finished the Ashes series at the top of the England batting averages and second in the bowling, I naturally assumed he would be included in the squad to tour South Africa. Anybody who knew anything about cricket could see he would be an automatic selection.

A major problem arose because Basil was classified as 'coloured'. Of course, that should not have been any kind of problem at all. So far as the South African team was concerned, we were looking forward to playing against Basil and the rest of the England team. There were no other issues.

However, the politicians got involved and various messages were conveyed to the MCC that the team would not be welcome if Basil was selected. Shamefully, one South African company tried to get around the problem by offering Bas a ten-year contract worth £40,000, a fortune in 1968, to coach in South Africa, if he declared himself unavailable for England. To his great credit, Basil stayed true to his principles and declined.

The England touring group was announced in August 1968, and Basil was not included. It seemed as if the England selectors had bowed to political pressure from South Africa. Quite rightly, in my view, they were criticised because, in pure cricketing terms, Basil had done enough to secure his place.

Controversy raged on all sides and a month later the MCC were given an opportunity to correct their error when Tom Cartwright suffered an injury and withdrew from the tour. They did the decent thing and, even though they were replacing a bowler with a batsman, Basil was named as the replacement.

That announcement sparked uproar in South Africa, which culminated in a speech by the Prime Minister John Vorster, where he denounced the MCC team as the 'the team of the anti-apartheid movement'. The England tour was cancelled and, all of a sudden, we realised we were in trouble.

I blamed the 'Nats', the Nationalist Party government that had ruled South Africa since 1948, and developed the system of apartheid where black people were treated like second-class citizens. I was only a young sportsman whose mind was full of playing cricket as well as possible, but I knew enough about right and wrong to realise that apartheid was wrong. Goodness, how I hated the Nats and their stupid policies.

In those days, the black and coloured South Africans who came to watch cricket had to sit in their specially designated stands, away from the white people. It had always been that way, but I hated the idea of division and, to be honest, I understood when some and black and coloured fans cheered whatever team we were playing. If I had been in their position, I would have done the same.

I certainly didn't feel as though I was a member of some white master race, and I hated the idea that, by playing cricket for South Africa, some people would see me as representative of the system. The truth was that I took no pleasure in listening to *Die Stem*, the national anthem. It just made be feel very sad, because the words seemed to celebrate a country, whose government had quite deliberately and cruelly robbed so many millions of its own citizens of their basic human rights. I found it very hard to accept.

Yet, I suppose, I was just a cricketer and, rightly or wrongly, I reckoned my job was to prepare myself as well as possible and to play as well as possible, whenever we got the chance.

The MCC tour to South Africa in 1968/69 had been cancelled, but there remained a general confidence that our 'old friends' in world cricket would stand firm. The news that the Australians had agreed to add a tour to South Africa at the end of their five Tests in India during November and December 1969 was greeted with great joy. We had not played a Test for three years, and I was eager to be involved.

The Australians had beaten the Indians by three Tests to one, but they had endured a tough tour, and I remember reading how the team didn't look too healthy when they arrived at Jan Smuts airport in Johannesburg on 2 January, 1970. "The players looked haggard," said Alan McGilvray, of the ABC. "Their eyes seemed to be standing out of the heads and some of them actually looked yellow."

Graham McKenzie, their main strike bowler, had lost six kilograms in the sub-continent, and Alan Connolly was suffering from bronchial pneumonia. In contrast, we were all fresh, eager and raring to go. The difference in the physical condition of the two teams is often overlooked when South Africans remember this four-Test series, but it wasn't our problem. We just wanted to play official Test cricket, and do well.

As the series approached, I found myself embroiled in a keen debate over who should captain South Africa: according to the newspapers, the selectors faced a choice between Ali Bacher and me. Some accounts of this era have suggested I was desperate to be named as the skipper, but that's not true.

Throughout my career, if I was ever asked to captain a team, I accepted the job because I enjoyed the responsibility and relished the opportunity to put some of my ideas into practice. However, captaincy was very far from the reason I played the game. It was never the be-all and end-all and, in fact, it was never something that I actively sought. If it happened, it was fine. If not, it was no problem.

In the event, Ali was appointed to captain the team in 1969/70, and I was absolutely happy with that. At a team meeting before the first Test, former captain Trevor Goddard and I both made a point of telling him he could rely on our total support and we were as good as our word throughout the series.

We were a team, united by a hunger to succeed. From what we could tell, we seemed to have a strong side, with plenty of players who were repeatedly described by pressmen and players from other countries as being truly world class, but all these compliments meant nothing unless we played Tests, and won. We were committed and none of us needed any extra motivation after what Bill Lawry said in the newspapers.

The Australian captain made a series of bold and upbeat statements about his team's prospects. This kind of sabre-rattling is fine, so long as you back it up with performances. However, if the batsman you describe as the best in the world (as Bill hailed young Ian Chappell) then struggles to score a run, you end up looking foolish and your extravagant predictions are hurled back in your face.

Bill had a tough time during the tour, and the series result has been a millstone around his neck ever since, all of which is unfortunate because he's a personable and very decent man.

The South African line-up in this series is worth repeating because, for all the problems enveloping our country at that time, the image of this side performing at its peak stands out in the memories of so many. For those of us who were involved, however innocent, naive and unaware we may have been, this Test series would always be recalled as special. For us, they were the halcyon days.

Our batting was opened by an emerging young genius called Barry Richards in partnership with the veteran Trevor Goddard, followed by Ali Bacher at three, the maestro Graeme Pollock at four, yours truly at five, Lee Irvine at six. Then we had the wonderful all-rounder Mike Procter, and the inimitable Tiger Lance, followed by the wicketkeeper Dennis Gamsy, who was replaced by Dennis Lindsay for the third and fourth Tests.

Peter Pollock led the bowling attack, and was variously supported by the reliable Pat Trimborn, John Traicos from Rhodesia, off spinner Kelly Seymour and left arm slow bowler Grahame Chevalier.

Many people reckoned this group was the strongest team in the world at the time, and began to refer to the golden era of South African cricket. Well, our golden era may have been severely curtailed by political factors far beyond the control of mere cricketers, but at least we are able to reflect upon the 1970 series against Lawry's Australians and recall that while our sun shone, it shone brightly.

The first Test of the series was played at Newlands and, mindful that South Africa had not managed to win a single Test on this ground in 60 years, we may have been cautious at first.

Once Ali had won the toss, we batted and ground out a first innings that would be made to look pedestrian by the fireworks that followed. I worked hard and, aware of the importance of the occasion, set myself a target of 25 runs by lunch and then, carefully and without risk, to take it from there. In fact, I managed to score 127 in just over six hours, which was slow for me, but it did the job. The record books note this innings as my fifth Test century, and my fourth against Australia. I have always thought the Aussies brought out the best in me because they liked to play the kind of positive, aggressive cricket that I so much enjoyed.

Others chipped in and, as we scratched our way to 382, the general expectation of a closely contested series seemed close to the mark. Then our opening fast bowlers, Peter Pollock and Mike Procter, the veteran and the new star, the ideal combination, bowling in perfect tandem, delivered such a broadside at the Australian batsmen that, perhaps, they never really recovered. The tourists were dismissed for 164.

We could have forced the follow-on but, after some debate, decided to bat again and thereby avoid having to bat last at Newlands, where South African teams had failed so many times before.

Still, our batsmen struggled to settle and, bemused by the thoughtful spin bowling of John Gleeson, we could manage no more than 232 in our second innings. However, with our pace attack straining at the leash, an overall lead of over 450 seemed adequate. So it proved, as Procter raced in and took another four wickets. Australia were bowled out for 280 and, at last, we had broken the curse and won a Test in Cape Town.

As the series continued, we became aware that the SA Cricket Association had suggested a fifth Test match should be added to the schedule. They probably had their eyes on the revenue, and the Australian board agreed. However, some of their players, led by Ian Chappell, objected and demanded an additional Aus$500 per player to play a fifth Test. There was no agreement and therefore no fifth Test.

We didn't mind either way. In fact, we would quite happily have played a dozen Tests that summer, but the Aussies were weary after their visit to India and, in fact, I respected their stand. Looking back, this may have been the first time a Test team stood up to their officials, and prevailed.

These discussions provided the backdrop to the second Test at Kingsmead but, in truth, whatever the mental state of the Australians, it was immaterial in the face of the onslaught that followed. Where we had stuttered and stumbled in Cape Town, we threw away the shackles and flowed in Durban. The ground was packed to its capacity of 16,000, as we produced a compelling and maybe irresistible performance.

Ali again won the toss, again we batted first and Barry Richards opened the show. People say perfection is not a human condition, but Barry's batting technique was as near perfect as anything I have ever seen. I used to watch him batting in the nets, and study his footwork, his back lift, his stroke selection: everything looked so natural and easy. This particular morning in Durban he set about the Australian bowlers and, if they had not deliberately slowed the game down, he would have reached his century before lunch.

Richards stroked a chanceless and magnificent 140 in barely three hours, after which the spotlight moved to Graeme Pollock, who proceeded to play what was probably the innings of his life.

From the outset, he hit the ball in the middle of his bat, pounding it through the offside with the authority of a master carpenter driving nails into wood. He simply took control, and, as his teammates, we watched in wonder and admiration. At one stage, Graham McKenzie put four players in the covers, but Graeme stroked the ball past them with ease. Next, Lawry gave Freeman a 7-2 offside field, but the maestro still thundered the ball past extra cover, with the minimum backlift and follow through, and maximum power.

He reached his 50 inside an hour, and almost shyly acknowledged the rapturous applause.

If anything, Graeme's onslaught intensified. I remember one of the Australians telling me afterwards that it wasn't that tough in the field. "At least, we didn't have far to run," said Paul Sheehan with a grin, "because Pollock was hitting the ball so hard, it was rebounding 20 yards off the boundary fence."

He was unbeaten on 160 at stumps on the first day, and he continued to entertain another full house on the second morning, crashing the ball around the field, a genius in full flight.

Graeme eventually struck the four hundred and first ball of his innings into the hands of Keith Stackpole, and his masterpiece ended with his score on 274, of which no fewer than 172 runs were reaped in boundaries. It was the highest score ever made by a South African in a Test, eclipsing Jackie McGlew's 255 scored against New Zealand in 1953, and it had been an innings that will forever be cherished all those who saw it.

We declared our first innings at 622 for nine and for once Pollock and Procter didn't burst through the top of the Australian order. Eager to make a contribution to this team of stars, I sensed an opportunity and, bowling first change with Trevor Goddard, I managed to find some pace and movement.

Lawry was lbw for 15, Chappell was caught behind without scoring and Doug Walters was then caught by Traicos for nought, all in a blur of excitement, adrenalin and loud cheering. I had taken three wickets in the space of eight balls, helping to reduce Australia from 44 for nought to 44 for three.

All out for 157 in the first innings, forced to follow on, the tourists offered sterner resistance in their second innings, with Stackpole, Walters and Redpath each reaching 70, but 'Proc' kept battering away and it was he who polished off the tail, sealing a famous victory by an innings and 129 runs.

The momentum had swung decisively in our favour, and we would probably have walked to Johannesburg to play the third Test at the new Wanderers. Once again, Ali won the toss. Again we batted first and this time it was Barry Richards who caressed an elegant 65 in our first innings total of 279.

We then dismissed Australia for 202, with Peter Pollock taking five for 39, and took control of the Test with a commanding second innings total of 408, in which Graeme made another outstanding 87, I contributed 110, and Lee Irvine made a neat 73. Everyone was eager to do their bit. We were playing against Australia but, in a positive sense, we were also competing against one another, inspiring each other to set new standards. In this series the South African team functioned as every effective sporting team should.

Facing another daunting total of well over 400 in the fourth innings, the Australians subsided again, bowled out for 178. We had taken a 3-0 lead in the series, and almost seemed to be dreaming.

Trevor Goddard had claimed the last wicket, having Connolly caught by Richards for 36, and this seemed wholly appropriate. He had declared himself unavailable for the scheduled tour to England later in 1970 and, in what seemed to be a fit of pique, the selectors dropped him for the fourth Test.

I remember Trevor making this announcement in the dressing room and looking around at all these great cricketers, and seeing barely a dry eye. We were all amazed by the pettiness of the decision, but Trevor went out with a bang, taking his one hundred and twenty-third and last Test wicket with his very last delivery.

We had won the third Test match in Johannesburg by 307 runs, which became South Africa's largest winning margin in Test cricket, but the new record lasted for just a single match.

The fourth Test in Port Elizabeth ostensibly seemed a dead match, with the series already won, but there was nothing moribund about our performance.

Ali won the toss, remarkably his fourth success in four, and, again, he elected to bat. The Test proceeded to follow a pattern that must have seemed grimly familiar for the Australians.

Richards made 81 in our first innings of 311, before Pollock and Procter each took three wickets in restricting the tourists to 212. We then took control of the match, raising the tempo in the second innings, with Richards and Irvine each scoring a century in 470 for eight declared. Faced by a target of more than 500 to win, the Australians succumbed to the pressure and, as Procter seized six for 73, were dismissed for 246.

Victory was secured by a crushing margin of 323 runs, a new South African record, and, more significantly, we had completed a 4-0 series win, our first ever clean sweep. As players, we were cheered as heroes, with every member of the team sharing in the accolades of a delighted cricketing public.

Richards and Graeme Pollock were recognised as the geniuses among us. Goddard and Peter Pollock had proven themselves to be Test cricketers of the highest quality, although Peter suffered the minor disappointment of not being able to complete what would prove to be his last over in Test cricket, because he pulled a hamstring in the second over of Australia's second innings and was unable to continue.

His young new ball partner, Mike Procter, had demonstrated the wonderful talent and competitive spirit that would earn him respect throughout the cricketing world over the next decade.

Ali had captained the team with quiet, calm authority, and I had managed to chip in with the bat and ball at various stages of the series. Lee Irvine had batted extremely well and, neatly, the legendary Denis Lindsay had conceded not one single bye in what would prove to be his last four Tests.

History relates this team never played again.

As we sat in the dressing room at St George's Park and, together with a few of Australian players, toasted the series, we were all looking forward to touring England in the northern hemisphere summer of 1970. The MCC had said the tour would go ahead and, naively, we foresaw no particular problems.

However, the Springbok rugby tour to Britain in 1969/70 had been besieged by demonstrations and in the end our cricket tour to England was consumed by a growing international consensus to isolate sports teams from the land of apartheid. The news was disappointing, but not a complete surprise.

The South African tour to England was hastily replaced by a Rest of the World XI tour, and I was among the group of South Africans invited to join several West Indians and other international players in the touring group. I enjoyed the series but, in truth, the matches paled in comparison to the real cut and thrust of Test cricket, to which I had become accustomed over the previous nine years.

Nonetheless the matches were officially classified as first class, a ruling for which I would be eternally grateful because it was during the 'Test match' between the World XI and England at Headingley that I managed to take what proved to be my one and only first class hat trick.

The ball was swinging and seeming around all over the place on a typically overcast day in Leeds and, with all the elements in the bowlers' favour, the batsmen were jumping around.

Alan Knott was the first victim, when a ball pitched on middle and hit his leg stump. Chris Old, or 'Chilly' as we called him, was then bowled by a decent delivery that swung away, pitched on the off-stump, then cut back and hit leg stump.

With two down, the crowd were getting noisy and excited, and a batsman called Don Wilson approached the crease to face what was going to be the hat trick ball. I decided I would pitch the ball as near as possible to middle and off. Don played forward and the ball hit him on the shin, from where it lobbed up gently to short leg and Mike Denness, a substitute fielder, caught it.

The umpire slowly raised his finger, and I had my hat trick. My teammates were all over me, and I was delighted, but there were still two balls left in the over. The next ball did not find its mark but, the next delivery,

I managed to have Colin Cowdrey caught behind with another away swinger. Four wickets in the space of five balls curtailed an England fight-back and created an opportunity for us to win the game, which we duly did afterwards.

There is an amusing postscript to this saga. While having a drink with some of the England players after the day's play, I happened to mention that, personally, I didn't think Don Wilson had touched the ball before Denness took the catch.

Ray Illingworth, the England captain, was sitting nearby and he had heard what I said. He sat upright and, with his typically dry sense of humour, the blunt Yorkshireman said: "Aye, typical Wilson... he'd do bloody anything to get into Wisden!"

The end of the World XI series in England marked the end of my official international career. Looking back, I count myself extremely lucky to have played 30 Test matches, and to have had the chance to represent my country on tour overseas.

The real sadness was that the potentially great Test careers of cricketers such as Richards, Pollock, Procter and many others were suddenly cut short by factors beyond their control.

That was the reality, which players and supporters alike had to accept. In 1970, the curtain of international isolation fell on South African cricket, and it would not be raised for 22 years.

As T.S. Eliot might have said, by beating Australia 4-0, at least the Springboks had gone out not with a whimper but a bang.

Chapter Eight – Wilderness Days

International isolation crept upon South African cricket. Nobody just switched off the lights, and plunged our game into darkness. The process was more gradual, as official tours were scheduled as normal, then thrown into doubt, then confirmed, then threatened again and then cancelled altogether.

Time and again, our hopes were raised, and dashed.

Typically, one or other 'friend of South Africa', maybe a right-wing politician or a former player, would make some bullish statements about retaining sports contact, or about not allowing politics to interfere with sport, and everyone would get excited, and start preparing for the tour. Then, inevitably, there would be another big speech, or another crucial meeting, and the invitation would be withdrawn 'with regret'.

We were up, and then we were down, up and down, up and down, until, after a few years, probably by the mid-1970s, we began to realise that fewer and fewer tours were even being scheduled. The bleak reality was that the curtain of international sporting isolation had fallen on cricket, and we would not play any more Test matches until our government had abandoned and abolished the policy of apartheid.

In those days, such a development was unimaginable.

Then the lights did go out.

I was not bitter about the sports boycott, not at all. I understood why it was started and I whole-heartedly agreed and supported its ultimate goal, the end of apartheid.

That does not mean that, as a professional cricketer who just wanted to play cricket, I did not feel frustrated when my Test career was curtailed by factors beyond my control.

And it also does not mean that I did not get annoyed now and then… annoyed when well-intentioned sports officials in South Africa worked hard to integrate sport, often at great personal risk, and were rebuffed… annoyed when political opportunists jumped on the boycott bandwagon

… annoyed when many 'holier-than-thou' overseas governments singled out sporting isolation because it was an easy means to knock South Africa, but continued to allow their officials and businessmen to profit from trading with the 'apartheid regime'.

Yes, the overriding goal was absolutely correct. That is clear. Yet, the end should never completely justify the means and it should be remembered that the international sporting boycott of South Africa, launched in the 1960s and ended in 1991, was riddled with hypocrisy and double-dealing.

South African cricket responded to isolation as any householder might respond to a power cut. On one level, as sportsmen and sports officials, we did what we could to inspect the wiring and resolve the problem, integrating the game where it was possible within the laws of the country. Some of these initiatives may have been cosmetic and expedient, but very many were sincere and meaningful.

However, we were tinkering at the edges and it became clear that a lasting solution lay only in the hands of the government and the voters. To continue the analogy, the power cut had been caused at the point of supply, and there was absolutely nothing we, as mere users, could do about it.

So, confronted by the reality of darkness, South African cricket worked hard to sustain the domestic game during isolation and, every now and then, generate a shaft of light from the outside world.

In the 1980s, the South African Cricket Union, led by Joe Pamensky and Ali Bacher, pursued a policy of recruiting so-called 'rebel' tours by offering various international players enough money to defy their own Cricket officials and politicians, make the trip to play in South Africa and accept the inevitable bans that followed. An English XI arrived in 1981, followed by a group of Sri Lankans, then some West Indians and, finally, an Australian team.

There was no such programme during the 1970s, and it was left to well-meaning individuals or sponsors to light small candles of cricketing contact with the outside world. Into a vacuum of organisation and planning poured a variety of opportunists, philanthropists and some decent cricketers. Nobody ever really knew what was going on in a Wild West type of environment, but some tours slipped through the net.

Derrick Robins was well known in the game and in 1973 he took it upon himself to assemble some leading players and form a team that would tour South Africa as the 'Derrick Robins XI'. It was far from Test cricket but, beggars could not be choosers, and I remember getting very excited about the matches. In truth, my preparation for a full Test series would not have been that much different.

There were a series of Derrick Robins XI tours to South Africa, and the first included well-known players like Roger Knight, Bob Willis and John Hampshire. Barry Richards, Mike Procter, Andre Bruyns and Kenny McEwan all played for our team: we had some decent matches. On a personal level, I made the most of the opportunity and managed to score a century before lunch at Newlands, a rare enough feat.

The second Derrick Robins touring team included Brian Close, the formidable character from Yorkshire and England, and, significantly, two well-known cricketers who were not white, John Shepherd, from the West Indies, and Younis Ahmed, from Pakistan. Special dispensation was required for them to play in South Africa and to use facilities that, in those days, ridiculously, were reserved for whites only. This was granted and, however small the progress might seem now, it did feel terribly important at the time.

Inevitably, the matter of money was never far away from these ventures, and problems arose when some of our leading players heard that the Robins players were being paid to play and demanded to know why the organisers had assumed the South African team would be happy to play for nothing. We were generally made to feel like second-class citizens – the visitors were given cars to drive round in while we were left to make our own arrangements – and this kind of thing didn't go down well.

Brian Close wasn't happy either. He said he wasn't interested in playing anywhere except the Wanderers in Johannesburg because he and his team were going to get a share of the gate receipts and, according to him, that was only going to be a worthwhile sum at the largest stadium in the country.

There was drama on the field as well.

I was batting early in the match at Newlands and, soon after John Snow came on to bowl, I nicked a catch which John Tolchard caught at second slip. The umpire didn't raise his finger, so I just stood there. Snow and his fielders went wild, quite rightly, and abuse was being hurled in all directions.

Lee Irvine was batting at the other end, and, at the end of the over, he calmly walked down the wicket and told me that, in all honesty, he thought I was out.

"Don't worry, Lee," I said. "I'll get myself out."

Well, I tried. I swiped and swung at everything, getting top edges, bottom edges and inside edges, and they all seemed to fly into or over the boundary. Snowy got angrier and angrier. We were hurling insults at each other, and he started to send down a barrage of bouncers. He was a top class fast bowler and seriously quick, and I saw from the look in his eyes how much he wanted to teach me a lesson.

After a while, the umpire issued Snow with a warning for intimidatory bowling.

I was enjoying the contest, and protested.

"Don't do that," I called to the umpire. "He's not fast enough to intimidate me."

By now Hylton Ackerman had joined me at the crease, and he decided to join the discussion. Not looking forward to facing Snow himself, with a deadpan expression on his face, Dutchman announced: "Well, Mr Umpire, I happen to agree with you. It is intimidatory bowling, and it should stop right now."

There were other Derrick Robins tours, with more personalities and incidents. At one match, I remember the touring players were lined up to meet the President of the Republic of South Africa. For reasons known only to him and his entourage, Mr Fouché addressed some of these visitors in Afrikaans.

"*Ek sien die son het jou gevang*," he said to Barry Wood, as he told the red-faced Englishman how he could see that he had been caught by the sun.

Check the knickers… celebrating our victory over England, Trent Bridge, 1965

Life was good after we beat Australia 4-0 in 1970; here I am in high spirits with my wife Helen, who is holding our daughter Susan, and my son Craig

Preparing for a 1974 Gillette Cup match against Transvaal with a young WP bowler named Morné du Plessis, who later became Springbok rugby captain

The Province team of the 1970s developed a fantastic Team spirit. Celebrating our Currie Cup title in 1975 are, from the left, Stephen Jones and Attie van Niekerk. Denys Hobson stands on the right.

Looking serious, and accepting the WP Sportsman of the Year award in 1975

Lump in the throat time… Newlands always felt like home, my favourite cricket ground in the world.

In 1984, I was asked to be Chairman of the SA Cricket Players' Association, a role that often required me to conduct deep discussions with my mates, Peter Kirsten, on the left, and Peter Cooke, on the right.

I worked with Hansie Cronjé when I coached the Free State team in 1991, and found him to be one of the most gifted cricketers and one of the finest men I have ever met. Nothing that has happened since then has made me change my mind, and I will forever hold him in the greatest affection

There were some good times with the Transvaal team of 1992 and 1993, and we won some silverware as well

"And the same to you, sir," Barry replied, quick as flash.

Amid all the drama and uncertainty, amid all the recriminations and arguments, amid all the sadness and the missed opportunities, through the years of isolation, we still managed to laugh.

Chapter Nine – World Series Days

One day in 1977, completely out of the blue, I received a telephone call from Tony Greig, the England captain who had been born and bred in South Africa.

"Listen, Bunter," he said, "Don't sign a contract with anyone until we meet in Cape Town. I'll call you when I get there, and I'll give you all the details. Just don't sign anything."

It was all very mysterious and, to be quite honest, I had no idea what he was talking about because he had given not the slightest indication of what he wanted me not to sign, or to sign, or whatever. However, as good as his word, Tony did call when he arrived in Cape Town and said we should meet.

"It's going to be biggest thing ever to hit cricket," he said, "and I'll tell you about it tomorrow."

What on earth could he be talking about? I wondered.

We met as planned, and I could hardly believe my ears as this England captain, supposedly a pillar of the establishment, proceeded to outline plans for a cricket revolution, nothing less.

"It's going to be called World Series Cricket," Tony told me. "We will recruit cricketers from Australia, South Africa, the West Indies and England, and they will play in Australia. If you want to be involved, your contract will be worth Aus$25,000. Do you think you might be interested?"

Of course, I might be interested. By this stage, there was no prospect that we would play any kind of official international cricket and, to be honest, the news sounded too good to be true.

"OK," he continued. "I'll arrange for the promoters to contact you. When you come across to Australia, you will meet Kerry Packer. He's the driving force behind the whole thing. Bunter, I'm telling you, it's going to be a whole new world. They're talking about playing in coloured clothing under floodlights, and one of their slogans is going to be 'Cricket's never going to be the same'. Get yourself fit, and get ready to play some of the best cricket you have ever known and, for once, we're going to earn decent money."

I hardly managed to get a word in edgeways. Greigy's build-up certainly set me thinking, and my first instinct was to find out as much as possible, to discover if this adventure was for real, so I rang around all sorts of people, anybody I thought might know something or other. Nobody was talking. In the end, I reckoned I didn't have much to lose and, after much soul-searching, decided to throw my cap into the ring.

Soon afterwards, an article appeared in the South African Sunday Times, which alleged that Graeme Pollock, Barry Richards, Mike Procter, Denys Hobson and I had all signed contracts to play in a new cricket competition in Australia. There were no more details, but almost everything in the article was accurate.

Finally, on 9 May, 1977, it was announced that 35 of the world's leading cricketers had signed contracts to play World Series Cricket. The news stunned the game's official administration, and it quickly became clear that the establishment would fight the rebel venture with every weapon at their disposal.

I must say the WSC organisation was superb. I was flown to England, where I signed my contract and was asked to meet with Kerry Packer's lawyers, who had been hired to defend a series of writs that had been issued by the official administrators to try and stop the venture in the courts.

The antipathy between the two sides quickly escalated, and it was Greigy's bad luck that he took most of the flak. Some people would not accept that the England captain would have anything to do with a venture like WSC, and they branded him a 'traitor', a 'pariah', a 'coward', and much worse.

They did not understand the fundamental reason why so many of the world's leading players had signed this contract. It came down to money. Test cricketers were filling the grounds, starting to attract major sponsorship and television rights income, and they were still being paid a pittance.

Over and over again, I heard the old chestnut being repeated. "It's not fair," cricketers chorused. "Look what the world's top tennis players and golfers earn, compared to us."

Personally, I never regarded this as a valid argument because there are too many differences between team sports and individual codes, but there was absolutely no doubt that, prior to WSC, the sums paid to Test cricketers were ridiculously low. The English establishment admitted as much when, after insisting for weeks that it would be impossible to consider any kind of pay rise, they responded to the WSC announcement by giving the England players a dramatic increase in their salaries. It was too late.

The dispute eventually landed in the High Court, and Jack Bailey, the MCC Secretary and a very decent man, created a bit of a stir when he was being cross-examined. The Counsel was theatrically roaming around the court room, looking everywhere except at Jack as he asked his questions.

"Excuse me," Jack piped up, "who are you talking to?"

In the end, judgement was given in favour of Packer, giving a green light to his cricket plans. Within days we were flying to Australia, and, as they said, the game would never be the same.

The first year of World Series Cricket was characterised by Kerry Packer's determination that, whatever obstacles were put in his path, the competition would be a success.

When the Australian Cricket Board took steps to prevent WSC matches being played at the country's main cricket grounds, they congratulated themselves on pulling off a masterstroke because they reckoned there was no way the 'rebels' would be able to prepare pitches for Test match cricket.

Kerry Packer had other ideas. He instructed his people to create concrete baths as big as cricket pitches, fill them with clay, plant grass and even put electric heaters on either side, connected by wires that ran through the concrete. He hired the best people, who applied the latest science to everything they did.

The grass grew beautifully in these baths, and, whenever a pitch was required, a crane was brought in to lift the concrete bath onto the back of a lorry. It would then be driven to the ground, which the WSC people had been able to hire for the match, and another huge crane would lift it into position. These pitches settled very well and, in fact, they played without any problem. Yet again, the new WSC boys on the block had shown that, with a bit of creativity and a lot of hard work, anything could be accomplished.

So the matches were played, and the crowds turned up, partly because the WSC people were not prepared to sit back and simply expect the spectators to arrive, as the cricket establishment had done for years. Their idea was to package cricket as entertainment, and to get it into the market place with a whole range of new promotional concepts to sell the game, and actively promote WSC among Australians.

As WSC players, we were frequently asked to attend promotional days in shopping malls, where the public would be invited to participate in quizzes and competitions. Packer's genius was to create an environment where nothing was sacred, and where the game could change at an astonishing pace. Ideas were always welcome. Some didn't work, and were dropped. Many did work, and have been part of cricket ever since.

I remember one evening when a group of us were asked to take the field before a match and experiment with a yellow cricket ball. It seemed an odd request but we had been using a white ball in the floodlit matches and it had proved difficult to see when it became dirty and scuffed.

The WSC people wondered if a yellow ball could be the solution but, in the event, the slightly blue tinge of the light from the floodlights somehow seemed to blend with the yellow, and, as it travelled along the turf, the ball disappeared as it became as green as the grass. We reported our verdict and the organisers eventually opted to keep the white balls, and give the umpires pots of white paint to keep them white.

As the months passed, more and more people started to realise that WSC, the project that, according to the establishment, was going to 'ruin the game forever' actually introduced a range of innovations and revisions that would, in time to come, help save the game. Nowadays, even the most trenchant traditionalist would surely agree that Kerry Packer did much more good than harm to the sport he loved.

This human dynamo may have been motivated by a determination to secure television rights for Australian cricket, but the effect was that he took by the scruff of the neck a game that seemed stuck in the past and, in his own inimitable way, hurled it into a successful and profitable future.

One of his most important advisors was Richie Benaud, and, in my view, he could not have made a better choice than the man who had captained Australia against us in 1963/4. I had grown to respect his deep knowledge of the game during that series and, whenever we met in the years that followed, I would be impressed by his rare ability to speak and act in the best interests of cricket. He's a great man.

Packer paid special attention to ensuring World Series Cricket looked entertaining on television, because he knew it had to attract an audience on the small screen as well as in the grounds, and he cleverly hired a series of great former Test cricketers to provide expert match commentaries.

One of these was 'Fiery' Fred Trueman, who was never short of something to say and, on one occasion, he was holding forth about the restaurants with topless waitresses that were becoming popular in Australia. Fred told us all exactly what players of his era – 'real men' – would have done in such places.

Well, not long afterwards, a group of us were invited for dinner at one of these restaurants in Adelaide, and Fred came along as well. He was regaling us all with more stories from his playing days, completely oblivious to an attractive topless waitress who was leaning over as she served a round of drinks.

Fred didn't draw breath until one of the waitress's ample breasts brushed his cheek. The look of absolute horror that froze on his face was hilarious, and he hardly said another word for the rest of the night: so much for all the big talk about what he and his mates would have done in their youth.

I was supposed to play for the WSC World XI most of the time, but I mainly turned out for a team the organisers created that was called the Cavaliers. It included some players on the fringe of the main WSC teams, and some leading players recovering from injury, and its main purpose was to play in the country districts of Australia, taking World Series Cricket to people beyond the big cities. I was selected for the team, and then asked to captain and manage the side.

This proved a great opportunity for me, and I enjoyed my time travelling around some lesser-known places with the Cavaliers. The only drawback was that the added responsibility meant I wasn't able to spend much time with Helen and our children, Craig and Susan, who had been flown out for a holiday in Australia as an added benefit in my WSC contract. They had a great time at places like the Great Barrier Reef, while Dad slogged his guts out on far-flung cricket fields with some of the biggest names in the game.

One or two people have suggested the players didn't take WSC matches seriously. In my experience, that is complete nonsense. It was probably the highest standard of cricket that I ever played, and my Cavaliers team was frequently getting involved in hostile contests, where tempers frayed on all side.

There was one match where Lenny Pascoe, the Australian fast bowler, sent down so many bouncers at the opposition batsmen that a row erupted after the game and we had to lock our changing room door to prevent a full-scale brawl from breaking out between the teams.

It was never easy to keep so many big names and big egos happy within one team, and I quickly learned to approach every situation with patience and care, two qualities that were not always the most obvious elements in my approach to the game. I tried hard but one day when, with a match due to start, two of our West Indian players had still not arrived at the ground, there was no alternative but to replace them with substitutes. The two players turned up not long afterwards, and they lashed out at me, calling me a racist.

Nobody could overlook the implications of a row between a white South African and two black West Indians, and I was hauled before Kerry Packer himself to explain precisely what had happened. My version of events was accepted and I was cleared of wrongdoing, but it was a horrible experience.

One of the rural towns we visited during World Series Cricket was Wagga Wagga, and it became the scene for one of the most frightening episodes of my cricketing career.

The World XI had just arrived in Wagga Wagga, this place whose name seemed so quintessentially Australian, and I was relaxing in the sun, lying beside the hotel swimming pool, when our obliging manager walked up to me and asked: "Can I help? Is there anything you want in Wagga Wagga?"

"A couple of dirty women, a steak and some red wine," I said, cheekily.

"Righto," he replied.

Well, I had an outstanding steak for dinner that night, and the red wine was excellent. Soon after eleven, I decided it was time for bed, and I quickly fell asleep. It was almost midnight when I suddenly woke up and, to my horror, discovered a human body lying in bed beside me.

At least, I thought it was a body. I can never see a thing at night, so I reached out to get my spectacles to see exactly what was going on, but I succeeded only in knocking over the bedside lamp. Now, I had no glasses, no light and what I reckoned was an unidentified body lying beside me.

"Doesn't a girl get a drink around here?"

The body had spoken, and it was a woman.

I stammered back: "Sorry?"

"I'd like a cup of tea," she said.

That was easy enough and, when I returned with the cup, she was sitting up in the bed.

"So, what you are doing here?" I asked, apprehensively.

"I work for the Australian Defence Force," she relied, matter-of-factly, "but I come up here every couple of weeks because I need the extra money to put the children through school."

That was odd. Her reference to the army made me even more nervous. As a South African travelling abroad, for some reason, I felt as though I ought to be concerned about government espionage and such activities, even if they probably belonged in a James Bond film rather than real life.

Then this woman started talking about apartheid, and, at that precise moment, I became utterly convinced that I had become the victim of some kind of high-level political set-up. Now panicking, I began to search the room for hidden cameras, looking behind the curtains, half-expecting to find a man in dark glasses.

"This could get me into a lot of trouble," I told her. "Please leave now."

"I don't care about your troubles, mate," she said blankly. "I'm here to do my job."

"Please, just leave," I repeated, begging.

She declined, repeating that she had been given a job to do, and she was not prepared to leave until it had been done. This exchange continued for a while, with me begging ever more desperately for her to leave and her refusing to move... until she suddenly relented, got dressed, said goodbye and left my room.

I was thrilled and, hoping my troubles were over (but unable to feel absolutely sure because there was still no explanation as to how the woman had got into my room), I quickly showered, dressed and went back downstairs to see if any of my teammates were still in the restaurant. All the World XI players were there, finishing their meal. I immediately noticed Mike Procter was sitting in the corner, grinning broadly.

"Hi," he chirped. "Have you had a good evening?"

"Excellent," I replied, wondering what he knew.

Nothing more was said. I drank a glass of calming red wine before returning to my room, where I spent a particularly restless night, trying to work out what any spy would want with me.

We were due to be taken on a fishing trip the next day, and my state of bewilderment was not eased when various teammates kept approaching me and asking if I was OK. I was starting to become even more suspicious, but nothing more was said. The days passed, and we continued to play through the series.

More than a month after my mysterious midnight encounter, the night before we were due to return home at the end of the first year of WSC, Kerry Packer hosted a farewell function at the Commodore Hotel. The setting was beautiful, in a room overlooking Sydney harbour, and I was enjoying myself.

"Well, Bunter, was she nice?"

I wasn't enjoying myself anymore. It was Procter, and I instantly knew what he was talking about.

"I don't know what you mean," I said, playing dumb.

"Well, you did ask for two dirty women, steak and wine in Wagga Wagga, didn't you?"

I smiled nervously.

"So, how did the dirty woman work out?"

I smiled broadly, immensely relieved, and everything fell into place. As I realised Proc had organised the whole thing, I could have hugged and kissed him. It hadn't been a government plot after all. I hadn't got involved with some kind of spy. I was in the clear, and it was if this huge burden of fear had been lifted from my shoulders. Proc fell about laughing when I told him how I had thought the woman was from the Secret Service.

Needless to say, I was mercilessly mocked for a long time afterwards, by Proc, who never truly believed me that nothing had happened, and also by Greigy, who started to tap me on shoulder whenever we saw anyone in a uniform and say: "Be careful, Bunter. They're coming to get you."

My fears were completely irrational, of course. What secrets would any undercover agent hope to get from me? I didn't know any secrets. Yet even now this tale sends a shiver down my spine. Perhaps such paranoia was symptomatic of being a white South African at the time, in what seemed a dangerous and apparently antagonistic world. We never knew who to trust, or what to believe, whether people might be representatives of our own government or of any other.

The most important match of my two years with WSC was effectively the final in the second year, although the ever-innovative WSC promotional people were not content to call the match just a 'final'. It was billed in all the publicity as the Supertest Grand Finale, between Australia and the World XI.

A cheque of Aus$61,000 was waiting for the winning team and, as I prepared to bat against Dennis Lillee in his prime, for no particular reason, I decided to wear a protective helmet for the first time in my career. It didn't do me any good, because I was caught in the slips, bowled Lillee for nought in the first innings and then bowled by the great Australian fast bowler for another duck in the second innings.

I blamed the helmet for this double misfortune, and was pleased that I had contributed at least something to our five-wicket victory by taking a decent catch in the Australian second innings.

Looking back, I remember my two seasons with WSC as an exhausting but fulfilling time. I doubt whether so many cricketing superstars have played in so many rural towns over such a sustained period of time as they did with the Cavaliers, and I genuinely felt it was a privilege to be involved.

Most of the WSC innovations seem old hat now, but youngsters never cease to be amazed when I tell them about the time when cricketers only wore white flannels, and only used a red ball. Well, I say, those were the days before a man called Kerry Packer dragged the game, kicking and screaming, into the modern era.

Chapter Ten – Province Days

Western Province cricket will always be very close to my heart. The combination of beautiful Newlands, my teammates through the 1970s and what we achieved, made it very special. I count myself extremely fortunate to have played for Province from the 1968/69 season, when I first arrived in Cape Town, through until the 1980/81 season, with just those two seasons away at World Series Cricket in between.

It was a long stint, and some people have been kind enough to give me credit for galvanising a team that was languishing in the B section of the Currie Cup. Well, that is very generous, but the truth is there were many people involved in the awakening of WP cricket, and I was lucky to be among them.

In my mind, it all started with Newlands Cricket Ground. It's not an exaggeration to say I felt inspired to work harder and play harder virtually every time I arrived at the ground. The sensational location, with Table Mountain as a backdrop, and the history made it a place where you wanted to succeed.

Newlands is still called the most beautiful ground in the world, and I think that is very close to the truth. At risk of sounding like a grumpy old man, I think it was definitely the case when all the oak trees were in place, but modernisation has brought plastic and chrome, and changed the character of the ground. There was a great hue and cry when the oaks were dug up, and some have been put back, but it's not the same.

In any event, it remains a special place, and that is precisely what I found when I arrived at the start of the 1968/69 season. Stellenbosch Farmers' Winery had offered me an excellent job as sales manager in the Western Cape, and I was obviously keen to play cricket for Western Province.

My first thought was that the team needed a positive approach. There was no shortage of gifted cricketers, but nobody seemed upbeat about our chances of getting out of the B section and putting Province back at the top of domestic cricket in South Africa. In my upfront way, I remember blurting out that everyone's attitude would have to change. People probably reckoned I was cocky, but 90 per cent of achieving anything is believing you are going to achieve, and the team didn't look as though it believed things would get better.

Recovery started at the top. I only knew one member of the Board when I arrived, and that was a great man called W.B. 'Billy' Louw. We had first met as opponents in a big school rugby match at Loftus Versfeld in Pretoria, when he was a front-row forward in the Rondebosch Boys High side and I was playing for Pretoria Boys High. They had beaten us that day, but I always liked him and enjoyed his company.

Billy introduced me to the other members of the Board, and I soon realised these were all decent cricketing men who had accomplished a great deal for the game. The fact is they had quietly started to develop all facets of cricket in the Western Cape, gradually improving the structures at junior level and at club level, essentially laying the foundations for the provincial team to achieve some success on the field.

At any rate, we started to work hard and, by the end of the 1968/69 season, we had won promotion back to the A section of the Currie Cup. We were playing well and, importantly, enjoying ourselves. The WP cricket players of the 1970s were a competitive bunch who played with smiles on their faces.

If I think back to those days, the memories flow thick and fast...

Not many South African batsmen were comfortable with spin bowling in those years, and we were fortunate to have two bowlers, a left-arm spinner called Graham Chevalier and the leg-spinner Denys Hobson. When these two found their rhythm, taking advantage of a typical turning Newlands wicket on the last afternoon, almost anything could happen. There were so many occasions when we won games from nowhere, and people would rush into the ground for the last hour to watch us snatch another victory.

It was our spinners who played the major role in turning Newlands into such a fortress. We loved the place, but opposing teams began to dread their visits to Cape Town, and nobody was made to feel more unwelcome than our adversaries from the Transvaal. The rivalry that developed between WP and Transvaal sustained the spark in South African cricket during the years when the country was isolated from Test cricket.

There was virtually no money in the game at that time, and the fact that we all had our day jobs meant that cricket represented the 'fun' part of our lives. We always played hard, but the consequences of losing or failing did not seem as foreboding to us as they seem for today's frowning professionals.

I will never say cricket didn't matter to us. We wanted to win as desperately as anyone, before or since. But cricket was not our livelihood, so we were not scared of losing a game, or losing a contract or an endorsement and we played with a smile. This 'amateur' ethos generated a wonderful spirit in the game and among the players, and it created a platform for so many great characters and time-honoured stories.

Andre Bruyns was one such character. A No.3 or No.4 batsman and an excellent short leg fielder, he earned a reputation for being the Clown Prince of Western Province cricket.

One day, fielding at third man during a quiet phase of the game, he started to shove his hand deep down into his trouser pocket. The spectators in that part of the ground noticed what he was doing, and started laughing as his entire arm disappeared in his pocket. We became aware of a commotion, and turned around to watch Andre finally produce a red-spotted handkerchief from his pocket. He had cut away the lining of the pocket. People laughed, and there was even a ripple of applause. Can you imagine that happening today?

This was the kind of cricket we played: it was hard, and fun.

On another occasion, playing against Eastern Province, Hylton Ackerman and I were standing side-by-side in the slips, when suddenly we heard a voice from behind us shout out: "Hey, Ackerman, don't you know that Barlow is sleeping with your wife?" The chirp was made in what Capetonians recognise as a 'coloured' accent, and we just assumed it came from one of our more outspoken spectators in that corner of the ground.

Hylton didn't enjoy the comment, but he managed to keep calm and, even though we were becoming aware of some laughter and sniggering around the ground, we both decided to ignore the remark and not to turn around and look at the stand from where it came. So, it was only at the end of the over that we eventually glanced in that direction, and saw Andre Bruyns standing at third man with a grin on his face.

It was our own teammate, who had made the chirp, imitating the local coloured accent and, when they realised what was happening, the spectators burst out laughing, thoroughly enjoying the sight of a Province player happily taking the mickey out of his captain and vice-captain.

Almost every day's play at Newlands was enhanced by a burst of humour from the popular stands, and we enjoyed every one. There was one game, when I was getting on at the end of my career, when Omar Henry and I emerged from the pavilion to resume our innings after lunch and one of the crowd shouted out: "Look, here comes Ouma (Granny) Henry and Oupa (Granddad) Barlow."

We played hard, and we enjoyed ourselves.

One of the traditions in the Province team at the time was that each new player was required to undergo a kind of initiation before he could be considered a true member of the side and, one day at Newlands, a young man called Stephen Bruce made his WP debut, as twelfth man, and underwent his own rites of passage.

"Excuse me, captain," our debutant said. "What should I do at the drinks break?"

I assumed he would know that the normal procedure was for the twelfth man to bring out a tray full of glasses of water or maybe fruit juice, but he didn't seem to know that and I sensed here was an opportunity for Stephen to have his initiation, and for the rest of us to have bit of fun at his expense.

"Well," I replied, with four or five guys sitting around me in the dressing room, and each of us managing to keep a straight face, "you must go to every member of the team and ask them what they want. I'll have two ham sandwiches with mustard, and a glass of fresh orange juice."

Stephen was understandably desperate to make a good impression on his new teammates, so he went off to get a pen and piece of paper and duly wrote down what I had ordered.

"Hey Steve," said Hylton Ackerman, who was sitting next to me, "you know I'm a diabetic, so I think I ought to have just a couple of boiled eggs and a glass of milk."

The youngster wrote this down, and proceeded to run around the rest of the team, taking orders for a wide variety of cakes, sandwiches and various hot drinks on what was a blazing hot day. When we went out to field in the afternoon session, he had an hour to prepare all the food and drink.

Then, when the umpires called for the drinks break, Stephen walked onto the field accompanied by an attendant, with their trays laden down with all sorts of goodies. By the time he reached the middle, we had dispersed to all corners of the field, meaning he had to walk around delivering the various orders as each of us lounged in our own space.

It wasn't long before the spectators cottoned on to what was happening, and some of them started shouting out their own orders from the stands. Everybody had a good laugh at poor Stephen's expense, as he realised what was happening. Well, at least, he had survived his initiation.

As Province players, we felt very close to the spectators at Newlands, especially the regulars who would sit in the same seats for every home match, loyally supporting their team.

One of the most familiar characters in the crowd was a fellow known to all as Kojak, because he was as bald as the detective played by Telly Savalas in the American TV series of the 1970s. His frequent comments, usually bellowed from the section of the ground known as the Willows, were legendary at Newlands, and they often had nothing at all to do with the cricket, but he was a loyal supporter.

Kojak enjoyed a drink or two, perhaps some wine or another alcoholic beverage and one day he almost got into trouble when he annoyed a couple of young policemen. He probably went a bit far and, while I was fielding, I saw the policemen walking purposefully towards him and looking as if they were going to arrest him. That could have provoked trouble among the crowd, because Kojak was a hero among his community, so

I decided to walk over and intervene. He may not have been everyone's cup of tea, but Kojak really didn't mean any harm, and I asked him to relax and persuaded the policemen to let him return to his place.

As players, we knew these guys, the regular supporters. They were part of the family, and it seemed completely natural for me to stop the game and help Kojak out of an awkward situation. Again, it's hard to imagine a similar kind of thing happening in the intense, cocooned environment of modern cricket.

The Guru was another well-known fan. He proclaimed himself as some sort of mystic being, who would sit in the middle of the pitch before a match, waving his arms around, casting spells to ensure a WP victory. Of course, one day he did all this, and we did win, and he became an instant legend.

When there was no cricket being played, the Guru was usually to be found around the middle of Cape Town and, at one stage, with cricketers typically being superstitious creatures, some of the players started to believe it was bad luck if you happened to spot him around the centre of town. I remember how established WP batsmen used to sit around in the dressing room, discussing his influence on their form.

Garth le Roux had an early ambition to be a jockey, because he was a scrawny, skinny youth, but he arrived at Western Province as a strong young man, standing 6'3" tall, with all the physical attributes to become a world class fast bowler. In all my experience, I had never seen a better prospect.

His magnificent performances for Western Province, in World Series Cricket and then for Sussex in England more than fulfilled this early promise, but I don't take any special credit for predicting that Garth would become such a fine bowler. You see, I had insider information from his early WP days when his raw pace forced us slips to stand further back than we did for any other quickie, including Procter or Pollock.

My only contribution to his development as a fast bowler was, every once in a while, to call in his direction: "Don't change anything at all, but just try and bowl a bit straighter."

Another of our promising young fast bowlers excelled briefly before opting to channel his sporting talents into rugby, and became one of the most successful Springbok captains. I remember Morné du Plessis came with us on a tour to Rhodesia, as it was then; he bowled very tidily and took quite a few wickets, and then came out with a remark that cheered those of us, old dogs, fielding in the slips. "I like bowling in this side," Morné said, "because when the ball is caught in our slips, it sounds like it has hit a wall of putty. Everything sticks."

The name stuck and, from then, our slip cordon was known as the 'Wall of Putty'.

Our wicketkeeper was Gavin Pfuhl. He was renowned for not being too keen on our fitness training, and one evening he came to a practice session with a sick note from his doctor, explaining that he had heart problems and should avoid too much physical exertion. There wasn't much for me to say and so, while the rest of us started our programme of exercises and running, Gavin headed for home.

Something didn't seem quite right, so, at the start of the session, I called the guys together and told them we were going to set off on a jog, and, without telling them, I led them down the road to where Gavin lived. Without bothering to ring the doorbell, the entire squad ran straight in to his living room, where our wicketkeeper had settled into an armchair with a cold beer. We then formed a circle around him, and watched him work through his physical jerks. Gavin didn't live that day down for quite a while, but he was a top class wicketkeeper and a great teammate.

Harry Bromfield was our off-spinner, and the butt of many pranks within the team. Just before one trip to play Transvaal in Johannesburg, a young Province batsman named Gerald Innes called Harry to one side and told him that Jo'burg was a long way from Cape Town and 'uphill all the way'. Gerald was a joker by nature and, with a deadpan expression, he proceeded to explain to Harry that, on account of the 'uphill' slog, the plane was not able to take as much luggage as usual, so we would all have to travel light.

Sure enough, the next morning at Cape Town airport, Harry turned up with a tiny suitcase, and was greeted by roars of laughter from his teammates. We took the mickey out of each other pretty relentlessly, but it was all meant, and taken, in good spirit. In every sense, that WP team was a family.

Johnny Farrell was a top class left-arm fast bowler but 'Boots', as we all knew him, had a tendency to move from his appointed fielding position. This proved particularly irritating for me, as captain.

In one particular match at Kingsmead, we had Boots firmly positioned at mid-on and, when the Natal opener on-drove the first ball of the match, I was not concerned… until I saw that Boots had drifted to his right, and the ball sped away to the boundary. My choice of language in communicating my feelings to Boots was less than pure and, at the end of the over, I told him to make a mark in the grass where I asked him to stand, and then to make sure he returned to stand exactly on that mark before each ball was bowled.

We changed ends, and went through the same rigmarole to make sure Boots had his mark in the grass at the opposite end as well. That, I hoped, would solve the problem. Not long afterwards, the bowler ran in … another firm on-drive, four more runs. Boots had wandered towards mid-wicket all over again. He was such a nice guy, it was hard to get too annoyed, but I was just about at my wit's end.

"Make your cross and stay where I put you," I shouted across at him.

Back came the reply: "I am on my cross, Captain."

"You can't be," I said, "otherwise you would have stopped that one."

"No, captain, I was there."

"On the cross?"

"Yes, captain."

The situation was becoming ridiculous, so I marched over and asked him why he found it so difficult to stand in one place. He pointed at his cross but, when I looked around, I saw somebody had marked out half a dozen other crosses.

It transpired that Peter Swart, fielding at mid-wicket, had seen what was going on and crept over to make a few crosses of his own in the grass. Poor Boots was completely lost.

Swartie is now in my Heaven's XI but nobody who knew him as a friend and teammate will ever forget him. He was always up to some kind of mischief, and it often involved taking his clothes off. The President of Western Province cricket in this era was Boon Wallace, whom we knew as 'Uncle Boon', and he didn't look too kindly on Swartie's sense of humour. After one of his exhibitions, on a bar towards the end of a function, as I recall, he was called to Uncle Boon's office and told this kind of behaviour was unacceptable.

I was present at the meeting in my capacity as captain, and I can recall Uncle Boon saying, with his familiar stammer: "Now listen Ch-ch-ch-chummy, this sort of ca-ca-ca-caper has to stop."

Two days later, we were playing in a six-a-side match at Groot Drakenstein, a beautiful little cricket ground near the Boschendal wine estate, just over the pass from Stellenbosch, and during the lunch interval I found myself sitting with Uncle Boon and his wife, Elizabeth, enjoying a quiet beer.

Our peaceful conversation was suddenly interrupted when two figures emerged from an orchard adjacent to the cricket field and pranced out towards the middle. Each of the men was carrying a large umbrella, and each of them, it soon became abundantly clear, was completely stark bollock naked.

"Ch-ch-ch-chummy," Uncle Book asked me, "wh-wh-wh-who is that?"

I hardly dared to tell him, but there was no option but to tell the truth. Dreading the outcome of my reply, I cleared my throat and said: "I believe that's Peter Swart and Norman Curry."

Uncle Boon turned purple and the veins on his neck began to stand out like ripcord. It was clear that Peter, together with his mate Norman, would be summoned back to the President's office.

Meanwhile the exhibitionists continued to dance around with their brollies, giving a performance that became known as 'The Mary Poppins dance'. Somebody called the security guards, but the spectators were enjoying every minute of this impromptu lunchtime entertainment, and Peter and Norman were left to complete their show before finally scampering back into the orchard, to a chorus of cheers and laughter.

Swartie was a fantastic character. During one of my WP team talks, I was telling the guys how we needed to get on top of the opposition, and go for the win. "Let's give them the *coup de grace*," I declared. Well, I could see Peter was listening hard and taking everything in and, during the course of the next game, he had everyone in fits of laughter when he asked: "Captain are we ready to give them the coup d'etat now".

What do you do when you are captain, and you have a player in your team who just seems to have been born naughty and is always getting into some kind of trouble? My view is you do nothing; you just relax, enjoy it, and duck when the flak comes. Swartie was that kind of guy and, as his teammates, we loved him for his upbeat approach to cricket and everything else. He had that wonderful ability to make people smile and, in a world when it often seems too few people see the funny side of life, that's a precious gift.

We enjoyed ourselves, but this Province team also played hard. Once we had been promoted back to the A section, our next target was to become established as one of the strongest provincial teams in the country and, as the 1970s ran their course, that is exactly what we did. A powerful batting line-up and a varied bowling attack was wrapped in a fierce desire to win, and we developed into a formidable team.

In fact, there were times when our competitive spirit caused problems. The traditional highlight of our season was the match against Transvaal, starting at Newlands on New Year's Day, when the ground would be virtually full. Emotions were always running high on these occasions.

One year, just before stumps at the end of a long, hot day, Mike Procter bowled a bouncer at Lee Irvine. The ball struck the Vaal batsman on the chest and, so it seemed to us, nicked his bat before being brilliantly caught by Andre Bruyns at short-leg. We all appealed loudly, but Lee stood his ground and the umpire gave him not out. We were livid, and some harsh words were exchanged as we walked off the field soon afterwards

That should have been that, but the insults continued. Tempers flared, the confrontation escalated and at one stage it looked as if there was going to be a full-scale fist fight between the Province team and the Transvaal players inside the pavilion at Newlands. The situation nearly turned very nasty, but we managed to keep the most fiery characters apart and everybody eventually calmed down.

That incident was a one-off, thank heavens, and I never witnessed anything similar. Cricketers, especially modern professionals, have an obligation to respect the traditions and etiquette of the game, and show discipline and restraint when emotions run high. I know all about the frustrations when poor umpiring decisions go against you, but you simply have to accept it and get on with the game.

In the early 1970s, it wasn't only the umpiring that riled South African cricketers. Even after the D'Oliveira Affair and the cancelled tours, many of the players still harboured a hope that somehow the Springboks might be able to play a few official Test matches, or even an overseas tour, now and then.

Such hope proved to be completely forlorn, of course, but, back in 1971, I can remember the enthusiasm when the South African Cricket Association made a formal request to the Nationalist government to include two non-white cricketers in the touring group scheduled to tour Australia that year. This seemed like progress and, if permission was granted, we reckoned the tour could possibly go ahead.

"No," said the Nats.

That was that.

To us as players, the decision seemed like the final nail in the coffin of our international Test careers and, as a group, a decision was taken that we would make a gesture of protest.

I was unfortunately away on a business trip to New Zealand, and missed what became widely known as the 'Newlands Walk-Off', but I publicly supported the cricketers who registered their protest against the government in a way that may seem mild now but was, at the time, extraordinarily brave.

A high-profile match had been arranged to mark the tenth anniversary of the founding of the Republic of South Africa, and it was agreed that Transvaal, the Currie Cup champions, would play the Rest of South Africa at Newlands. This occasion provided the platform for the players to take action and, in the greatest secrecy, a plan was developed, discussed, accepted and implemented.

Mike Procter opened the bowling for the Rest of South Africa and, after just one ball had been bowled, much to the surprise of the spectators in the stands, all the players proceeded to leave the field. Peter Pollock then took a prepared statement and distributed it to the journalists sitting in the Press Box.

The declaration read: "We cricketers believe the time has come to express our views. We fully support the South African Cricket Union's application to include non-whites on the tour to Australia, if good enough. We also subscribe to merit as the only criterion for selection in any cricket team."

The players then walked back to the middle, and resumed the game. This was earth-shattering stuff in a time when it was considered almost treasonable to oppose the government, but at least those cricketers who had the courage of their convictions can look back on the protest with some pride.

At any rate, somehow managing to control our frustrations when umpiring decisions went against us, and gradually accepting the reality of complete international isolation, we played some pretty decent cricket through the 1970s and, more often than not, sent the Province fans home with smiles on their faces.

All things come to an end and looking back, I suppose things were never really the same after I returned from spending a couple of summers playing World Series Cricket in Australia. Nothing ever stays the same in life, or in cricket, and the team appeared to have moved on. I didn't particularly enjoy the 1980/81 season in the WP team, and started looking around for a new challenge at the end of my career.

There was one last challenge for me at Newlands, and that was to help Province take the first steps on the road to fielding a fully professional team. We had all been semi-professional cricketers with day jobs and, if you were lucky, understanding employers who allowed you leave to play, but now the ripples of the Packer revolution were being felt in South Africa, and the major provinces started to turn professional.

I managed to help secure a team sponsor for Western Province for the 1981/82 season, which would facilitate the transition and enable the province to pay the players properly but I decided not to stick around and share in the windfall. Three of us – Peter Swart, Stephen Jones and I – looked at the situation and agreed to leave WP and play for the Boland Cricket Union, another province based not more than 40 miles from Cape Town.

Boland were playing in the B section of the Currie Cup, but they'd been promised by the South African Cricket Union that, if they won the B section, they would be promoted to the A section. That was precisely the kind of challenge I relished. Stephen Jones was also enthused, to the extent that he gave up his benefit year at Western Province to join the Boland crusade. Ted Wicht was the President of Boland Cricket at the time and, when we heard his plans for the future, we quickly recharged our batteries and signed up.

I still have the Boland team photograph from the 1981/82 season, and I have to say we looked like a bunch of hippies. We all had ridiculously long hair, and Swartie had his Che Guevara moustache. The following season's team photo looks exactly the same. I suppose that was the fashion at the time.

There were a few obstacles, most notably the reality that Boland cricket didn't have a home ground, but we played our matches at the SFW ground in Stellenbosch and started producing some decent cricket. We became a successful and happy team and, what was even better, we were a multi-racial team.

John Hendricks, Charles Hendrickse and Howie Bergins came from the Stellenbosch area and were officially classified as 'coloured', and they were all important members of our team. I was so fed-up with all the talk about colour and divisions. We were just a bunch of cricketers. That was all there was to it.

At one stage, we went on tour to South West Africa, later to become Namibia, and I remember a blazing hot afternoon when the Boland players were lazing around the dressing room.

"Look at this," one of the SFW guys who had helped organise the trip suddenly declared. "I don't know why people worry about whites and coloureds playing together. This is perfect."

"No, it isn't," Howie Bergins interrupted. "It's us darkies who have to do all the bowling in the heat, and the whiteys are only interested in the batting. It's just like the old days."

He was smiling broadly. Everyone laughed. It was a great moment. I had always reckoned that as soon as we South Africans could start to laugh at themselves, we would start sorting out the problems that prevented our country from realising its potential. Humour is always a great healer.

Not many people were aware that this Boland side and, to a greater extent, the SFW club team that most of us played for, enjoyed the enthusiastic support of a man called Basil D'Oliveira. Dolly used to come and watch us play on his regular trips back to visit his family in Cape Town, and it was fantastic to have him back in circulation in local cricket. I always marvelled at his balanced approach to the whole situation.

Well, Boland won a few matches and, to our delight, we achieved our target of winning the B section, known as the Bowl. Our promised promotion to the Currie Cup proper was, we assumed, a formality.

No, it wasn't. The SA Cricket Union reneged on the deal – as I recall, we read about their change of heart in the newspaper. So many people had worked so hard, this was difficult to accept and our desperate requests for an explanation were ignored. Boland cricket, it became clear, would have to be satisfied with playing in the B section and taking some reflected pleasure when the players they developed moved on to succeed elsewhere at the highest level of the game.

Boland was finally promoted to the Currie Cup more than a decade later, when the new United Cricket Board of South Africa took a strategic decision to expand the base of the game. A superb new stadium was built on the old Paarl showgrounds and, I like to think, the seeds we sowed in 1981 finally yielded some fruit.

I played through a second successful season with Boland in 1982/83, and was delighted by the enthusiasm of players who, though clearly devastated by the SACU's broken promise of promotion, still turned up and trained as though they were preparing for a full Test series against Australia.

At the end of that campaign, approaching my forty-third birthday, and with my body starting to ache, I decided it was about time the old man stopped playing cricket and did something else.

South African cricket had by this time entered the era of the 'rebel' tours, and the arrival in South Africa of players from England, Sri Lanka and the West Indies, all clearly being paid a great deal of money, provoked more discussion among local players about their wages and contracts.

Somebody came up with the idea of forming a Players' Association to represent the interests of the South African players and I was asked to serve as chairman. I wasn't sure about the wisdom of this choice, because the chairman would have to lead negotiations with the administrators and, so far as I was aware, over the course of my playing career, these gentlemen had always regarded me as awkward and abrasive.

Anyway, I was asked to do the job, and I agreed.

The first bone of contention was the issue of fines. The administrators wanted the right to impose fines of as much as R2,000 on any player who said anything about the game or rebel tours which they considered damaging to the game of cricket. I believed this was excessive, a sentiment that was reinforced when I was driving along the street in Durban and saw a newspaper billboard reading: 'MURDERER FINED R1,800'. A series of discussions was held, but the officials did not relent, and the players were not happy.

Then, one bright morning in 1984, I arrived at the Wanderers in Johannesburg to watch the South African team play against the unofficial touring team from the West Indies, captained by Lawrence Rowe. There was a big crowd, and I was just about to settle into my seat when I was startled by a voice over the public address system: "Would Eddie Barlow come to the home changing room immediately?"

I made my way to the South African changing room, and walked into a full-scale crisis. The players were refusing to accept the fines, refusing to sign their contracts and refusing to play the match against the West Indians. Voices were being raised. It was chaos.

Phone calls started going back and forth, and the scheduled start of play was drawing ever closer. This was getting us nowhere, so I decided a simpler approach might solve the problem.

"Listen," I said, taking one of the contracts and turning to the page with the clause about the fines. "All we have to do is cross off one of these noughts, and we can all agree on R200 as a maximum fine. Then we can sign the contracts and give these spectators what they have paid to see."

That was duly done, the players signed and the match went ahead.

In further discussions, I suggested future confrontations would be avoided if the Board simply withdrew the concept of fines. After all, I argued, if they ever wanted to punish a player for bringing cricket into disrepute, they simply had to drop him from the team. This principle was eventually accepted.

Once I had served my term as chairman of the Players' Association, I ceased to have any direct role within South African cricket until I started coaching in the early 1990s. The break from the game was welcome, after a provincial playing career that started in 1961 and ended in 1983.

There had been ups and downs... many more ups than downs, I am happy to report. It was a turbulent era, on and off the field, but overall, looking back, I consider myself to have been extremely fortunate to have played in so many great matches, and to have made so many lifelong friends in the game.

It wasn't a bad innings, not a bad innings at all.

Chapter Eleven – Derbyshire Days

Reflecting on the three seasons I spent with the Derbyshire County Cricket Club, the English summers of 1976, 1977 and 1978, I am tempted to leave the entire task to James Graham Brown, a member of the team who had a particular talent for writing clever and amusing poetry.

James wrote a poem about my period with Derbyshire, and he stood and read it out at a function to mark my departure from the club in September 1978. It was rapturously received by everyone who heard it, and I have included the entire poem in the Appendix at the back of this book.

The opening verse sets the tone:

> *There was once a Derbyshire Sec*
> *Who saw that his club was a wreck,*
> *So to hold the ship steady*
> *He sent for King Eddie*
> *Then went to the bank for the cheque.*

Well, I suppose that was true. Derbyshire cricket was not in a great way when I arrived at the club at the start of the 1976 season in England, but I didn't have much time for the headlines that suggested 'WORLD CLASS PLAYER ARRIVES TO REVIVE DERBYSHIRE'. If we were going to achieve anything, it was going to be done by each and every player in the squad, and the back-up staff. We needed to be a team.

I had wanted to play county cricket for some time but no one had ever asked me before and I always seemed to be busy doing other things. So, when an opportunity to play for Derbyshire arose, I didn't hesitate. It turned out to be one of the most rewarding episodes in my career. I learned a lot, and I thoroughly enjoyed myself as well.

The first task was to change the attitude of the players. It didn't take long to realise the Derbyshire team included some top-class players – Bob Taylor, Geoff Miller and Mike Hendrick – but, as a unit, they appeared to lack self-belief. My intention was to get the team enjoying their cricket and, as a result, I was sure they would start to feel better about themselves and produce improved performances.

This theory holds good in just about everything, whether it's county cricket or business: if people are able to enjoy what they're doing, it usually follows that they will be successful.

At Derbyshire, we needed to start playing aggressive, positive cricket. If we did, I felt confident we would start winning matches. This had to become the team's philosophy. As team captain, I saw it as my responsibility to provide a definite sense of direction, so that, whatever happened, each individual could carry on with his own game, sure in the knowledge that another seventeen or eighteen guys were right behind him.

My view was that winning is a skill that needs to be learned. It is a state of mind, an attitude that can start with one or two individuals and spread through a team. That's what needed to happen with us.

"Some teams seem to know how to win, others don't," I told the players at one stage. "I have seen games that should have been won, lost by teams that did not know how to win. When the opportunity presented itself, they did not see it and they were not capable of handling the situation. If we are aggressive and positive, if we all understand what we are aiming for, we will develop this capacity to win."

I hoped I was making myself understood. I wasn't sure, but I felt as if I had been hurled in at the deep end and the only way I was going to swim was by using the strokes I knew.

Physical fitness was another element of the plan. There didn't appear to be a proper training programme in place when I arrived at Derbyshire, or anywhere else in England, as I was soon to discover, so we soon established a schedule of sprints and exercises to get the players fit for the coming season. Some of these sessions took place at the Baseball Ground, home of the Derby County Football Club, and they aroused considerable interest in the media. The BBC sent their cameras and produced an item that was entitled: "Sports Day at Derbyshire CCC." Within a few weeks, the squad was fit and we looked like a professional team. It was hard work, but the process helped to build team spirit as well.

I could not have asked for a better response from the players. They had grown accustomed to playing cards and relaxing when they weren't actually playing, but now they were being subjected to a rigorous fitness regime. Some of our opponents would laugh when they saw us starting our physical jerks before matches, but they were not smiling a few days later when we had given them a hiding.

We worked hard as a team, enjoyed ourselves as a team, and improved as a team. "Oh well," Mike Hendrick remarked after one tough training run, "if we ever come up against a batsman who hits the ball out of the ground, we will certainly be able to fetch the ball more quickly than any other side." And everybody laughed, and paused a moment, and then set off on another run, with 'Hendo' leading the way.

By and large, the English counties look after their overseas players extremely well, and the good people at Derbyshire could not have been kinder to the Barlow family when we arrived. We were provided with a house in Lilleymede Close, in Wingerworth, near Chesterfield, within walking distance of an English corner shop, where it seemed everybody was friendly and you could buy just about anything.

Living from April till September in Derbyshire, and then from October till March in Cape Town may have been a life of perpetual summer, but it did present challenges for Helen and the children. Craig and Susan enrolled at the Rother Junior School, which was fine, and Helen did a great job teaching them at home, ensuring they kept up to date with the different curricula at their schools back in South Africa.

Otherwise, we enjoyed the English way of life: milk delivered to the doorstep each morning was a revelation, and visits to the local 'chippie' (fish and chip shop) were always enjoyed.

I recall there was a small river running down the side of our garden, and a small, old stone bridge where we used to sit and watch, among other things, a family of rats emerging from the undergrowth to sun themselves on the riverbank. It was like Wind in the Willows, in real life.

There are wonderful characters to be found in every English county, where the history and tradition seem to have seeped into every weathered stand and wooden seat. Derbyshire was no exception.

Phil Russell was our coach and he took great delight in giving instructions that wickets should be prepared to suit our pace attack. For one important match against Warwickshire he produced a wicket with a nice green tinge that suggested it would be lively. The visiting team had a look, and weren't impressed.

"That grass is green," the Warwickshire captain said warily to Walter, our wonderful groundsman.

"Aye," came the classic reply, "all bloody grass is green!"

Our changing room erupted in laughter when we heard what had happened, which was great. Just like the WP team back home, I wanted our side to have fun and play hard. That was the way it seemed to work for me: enjoy yourself, and the results would follow. I think teams can come unstuck if they set winning as the first and only goal, and forget to have a bit of a laugh along the way.

Mind you, no team with somebody like Fred Swarbrook, our left-arm spinner, in its ranks was ever going to have too much difficulty finding reasons to smile and laugh. There was one period when, as cricketers say, Fred completely lost it. In one limited overs game, he bowled a ball that flew over the wicketkeeper's head and then a delivery that trickled up to the batsman. Everybody was offering him advice and trying to help, from giving him a double brandy before the game to telling him to carry a lucky pebble in his pocket.

Nothing seemed to work.

"OK, Fred," said Bob Wincer, an exasperated teammate, as another delivery landed wide of the mark, "just put the cricket ball in your pocket, and try bowling the damn pebble."

Tony Borrington was our substitute wicketkeeper, and the type of character that made our team tick. He had actually been released the previous season, but was re-employed after I arrived. Keeping wicket in a match against Oxford University at The Parks, he suffered a deep wound when one of the Oxford batsmen attempted a hook shot but he missed the ball and it hit him on the head with his follow through.

Borrers was immediately taken to hospital for stitches, but he returned to the ground a couple of hours later and told us how he had met a beautiful blonde nurse, and had arranged to meet her that evening. His 'date' was vetoed at a team meeting, when the rest of us decided he'd had enough excitement for one day.

Many observers judged Bob Taylor as the outstanding member of our squad, and I agreed with them. In my experience of top class glovemen, Dennis Lindsay was a more prolific batsman but, judged purely on his brilliance behind the stumps, I reckon Bob was the finest wicketkeeper of them all.

The first time I saw him play was when he joined an International Cavaliers tour to South Africa in 1976. We had never seen such class before. He was so neat and efficient, setting about his work without any wild histrionics or unnecessary diving. Standing up or standing back, he was a genius. It was a pity he played in the same era as Allan Knott, or he would have shone in many more Test matches for England.

Bob was an important calming influence in the dressing room, although I recall he did get irritated when some of the youngsters got up to their tricks when we were playing away games and started moving his shoes around or hiding his newspaper. They were just having fun, but Bob said it was 'childish and unnecessary'. More laughter followed.

It was my honour to succeed Bob as captain of Derbyshire. He didn't much enjoy the job, and said he would prefer to focus on his 'keeping. I was pleased to accept the responsibility, and enjoyed the challenge of leading a new team in new formats of the game in what was a new environment. Going to Derbyshire may have been a step into the unknown for me but, in many ways, the change revived my career.

One aspect of this new situation was the weather. English people used to call April and May Spring. Well, for a South African shivering on a cricket field in Derby as the winds whistled down from the Pennines, it felt more like an Arctic winter. Local players dressed accordingly, wearing as many jumpers as possible, an item of clothing called 'long johns', which were ankle-length underwear, sometimes balaclavas and, once or twice, ladies' tights. That last option was not always popular but, as the racing fraternity are aware, silk retains the warmth very effectively.

However, when a young South African batsman called Peter Kirsten

Cally and I liked this photograph so much, at our farm near Robertson, with our dogs Sooty and Sweep, that we used it for our Christmas card that year

Coaching Bangladesh, standing with Gavin Benjafield, a fellow South African and the team trainer. "We'll just stand here while they run round," I seem to be saying.

Bangladesh was full of enthusiasm for cricket, and I enjoyed the challenge of moulding a national team. This was the official team photograph, 1999

After my stroke, Cally and I settled in Wales, and I was delighted to coach this happy bunch, the North-East Wales under-13 team

arrived at the club, he decided this kind of dress was not for him. Unforgettably for all who watched, 'Kirsey' was undaunted by the weather and set off for his early morning jog dressed as if it was a hot summer's day in Cape Town.

When he returned to the pavilion a quarter of an hour later, he looked like some kind of ghostly apparition because his moustache had literally turned white with frost.

"Gee, it's cold here," he mumbled, as we took him to the bar for a heart-starter. There was no more T-shirt and shorts for him, and he was soon bundling himself up like the rest of us.

South Africans were generally welcome in county cricket, and, over the years, players like Mike Procter at Gloucestershire, Barry Richards at Hampshire, Clive Rice at Nottinghamshire, Ken McEwan at Essex, Garth le Roux at Sussex and others, all produced performances that not only endeared them to their adopted county clubs, but also reflected well on the enduring strength of South African cricket.

We were certainly motivated to play well because, during the years of international isolation, English county cricket represented just about the highest available level of the game. So we gave 100 per cent and, in return, I reckon that, with few exceptions, we were treated extremely well by our counties.

I certainly could not have asked for a more supportive Chairman than George Hughes, who took over the job at Derbyshire just as I arrived. He owned a company that made coaches, the metal variety with four wheels, and he quickly decided we would use one of his buses to transport the team up and down the country from match to match, on the six-days-a-week treadmill of English county cricket.

Some of the players were not too happy about this, because it meant they would no longer drive to matches in their own cars, sharing lifts and each receiving a car allowance, which historically represented an opportunity to save some pocket money. The long coach journeys were quite good for team spirit, and Phil Sharp used to be the quizmaster as we whiled away the miles, but the players were still annoyed.

A few of the guys decided to make their feelings known. During one trip, someone was pushed into a table, which promptly broke. Other 'accidents' followed, until Mr Hughes decided enough was enough, and sent a bill for the repairs with the instruction that the players should pay. I was called to a meeting with the Chairman, where this matter was discussed, and it was eventually agreed we would use our cars again.

David Harrison was an outstanding Club Secretary who was always looking for ways to improve conditions for the players. Charlie Elliott, a Test umpire, chaired a Cricket Committee that always seemed to be constructive and consistent. He often came into the changing room with a word of encouragement. John Brown ran the youth cricket with great passion and skill. All these gentlemen – for that is exactly what they were – contributed to the development of a positive mood around the club and, before long, a winning team.

By general consent, Derbyshire performed beyond all expectations in 1976, making decent progress in the limited overs Benson & Hedges Cup competition and holding their own in the County Championship. I felt we were on the right track, but there was clearly more work to be done.

The following year, carrying forward a strong team spirit, we spent more time developing individual players who had the ability to turn a match with a great innings or a devastating spell of bowling. Cricket is almost unique as a team game, played by 11 individuals, and we needed to develop on both levels.

One of our opening batsmen was a fellow called Alan 'Bud' Hill. His technique was pretty sound and he was able to occupy the crease but, at one stage, he had trouble scoring at a decent rate. So, I took him to the nets and told him to the hit the ball as hard as he could. The idea was that I would provide the full tosses and half volleys, and he would regain the sensation of bat smashing ball. This drill usually worked.

Whenever I had the same problem I used to take myself down to the driving range and hit the cover off some golf balls for half an hour or so. That also did the trick. Cricketers face all sorts of problems in their careers, and it's always useful to be aware of instant remedies that may have worked for others.

So the team continued to develop, and, as time passed, we worked hard to keep improving, assessing our strengths and weaknesses and, where necessary, we signed new players. I was particularly well served in this regard by the wise, blunt and knowledgeable counsel of three well-versed observers of Derbyshire cricket: Gerald Mortimer, Neil Hallam and Mike Carey, a journalist and a close friend. For me, working with the players on a daily basis, their perspective on areas where we could improve was often invaluable.

Mike was known by me as 'Bevington', because that was the pseudonym he used when he wrote articles for The Daily Telegraph, and he called me 'Baslow'. That name originated from a comical skit performed by Geoff Miller and Mike Hendrick, where the two cricketers acted as themselves seated alongside an elderly local man in a pub somewhere in the depths of Derbyshire, discussing cricket.

"Oose that new bloke ye've got oop ther," the old man asked.

"Oose that," Mike replied.

"Wot's 'is name? Baslow?"

"Oh, Lazlo Baslow?"

It went down well, and, for some time, I was known as 'Lazlo' to this trio of men, who gave so much of their time and expertise to the Derbyshire cause, making the rest of us look good.

Phil Russell, as coach, was chiefly responsible for maintaining the strength of the playing squad, and he did an outstanding job, keeping his ear to the ground and identifying potential signings. He often used to pipe up and whisper in my ear that he had found somebody special; then we would set off together to some far-flung field somewhere in Derbyshire where we would watch our next Bradman.

There was one time when he drove me to a village called Heanor to watch a batsman who he thought might strengthen our team. Well, we arrived early, and waited and waited, until eventually we set eyes upon a tall man with wild black hair, holding a cricket bag in one hand and a guitar in the other.

His name was John Wright, and he was a New Zealander. His team batted first and, as we watched from the boundary, he proceeded to launch a barrage of boundaries and sixes.

"Well, what do you think, captain?"

"Well done, Russ," I replied. "You've found our overseas player."

Wrighty became a much loved and wonderfully prolific batsman for Derbyshire, even though he did have one extremely peculiar habit. Cricketers used to keep all their kit in long rectangular boxes that they call 'coffins', and, sometimes at the end of the day, John would carefully remove his gear and proceed to lie down in his coffin, with his feet protruding from one end and his head from the other. He seemed to find this routine relaxing but, as the runs flowed from his bat, we would have forgiven him just about anything.

In 1977 we finished a respectable seventh place in the County Championship, with everyone playing a role in the general improvement of the team. We were a real team in every sense, but I do admit to taking particular pleasure in the progress of two Derbyshire players – Miller and Hendrick – who developed to the point where they became important members of the England Test side.

It had always been one of my goals to get as many Derbyshire players as possible into the England team, because I wanted our up-and-coming youngsters to see that, if they worked hard, made sacrifices and kept their minds on the task, they too could achieve the same honours.

'Mills' was a fine slow bowler, and he was also a huge help to me in the field, always concentrating on the game, providing me with a flow of constructive comments and advice. Such players are like gold dust for a captain because, when things are going against the team, far from sitting back and watching from their place in the field, they are talking to you, getting involved, trying to put things right. It was no surprise to me when Geoff became county captain and, much later, a successful and respected national selector.

'Hendo' was a truly magnificent swing and seam bowler, following in a strong tradition of great Derbyshire pacemen. His performances on the field were a major factor in our success, and he was also a positive, upbeat presence in our changing room. I remember he and Fred Swarbrook had this standard routine where, as soon as Hendo walked in to a room, Fred would jump up into his arms like a monkey.

The two of them would proceed to chatter away like a pair of chimpanzees. Such behaviour might seem odd on paper, but it regularly had the rest of us in stitches and, within the demanding routine of county cricket, where you are playing five or six days every week, team spirit is absolutely vital. This was our strategy: first, enjoy the game and have fun … and, as a result, play better and win. If fooling around like monkeys helped us get results, that was fine by me.

It had always been my plan that the 1978 season would be my last at Derbyshire, because three years was enough to be away from home, and I would have loved nothing more than to leave the players and the supporters with a trophy. For much of the year, it seemed this fairytale ending might be possible.

We made progress in the Benson and Hedges Cup, beating Lancashire and Gloucestershire on our way to a home semi-final against Warwickshire. It was an exciting time. Suddenly everybody in the town was talking about cricket and people were stopping us in the street to wish us luck in the big match.

I remember we arrived at the ground before the semi-final to find multi-coloured bunting everywhere and, as I looked at the anticipation and determination written across the players' faces, I realised we had come a long way since those early training sessions at the Derby County football ground.

There was no way we were going to lose. We wanted our place in the showpiece final, and we wanted our supporters to have their big day at Lord's. Sure enough, we beat Warwickshire by 41 runs, and the whole ground went mad with excitement. It was one of the happiest days of my career.

History records that Derbyshire lost the 1978 Benson and Hedges final to Kent. We batted first and, despite a brave innings by Peter Kirsten, could muster no more than 147. Kent were an experienced, clinical one-day team in those days, and they knocked off the runs easily.

So, Cinderella had not run off with her handsome Prince and lived happily ever after but, in our Derbyshire fairytale, by reaching a major Lord's final, it can be said that we had at least gone to the Ball.

Chapter Twelve – Farming Days

Even since I can remember, I have hankered after the life of a farmer. Cricketing commitments, initially as a player and then as a coach, were always an issue, and I often had to rely on others to help me through while I was away, but, ever since the mid-1970s, I variously tried my hand as a pig farmer, then as a sheep farmer and, eventually, as a wine farmer.

Not much beats the pleasure of working outdoors in a beautiful part of the world, and a farmer's life rarely seems to lack characters and peculiar challenges. It's never dull.

It all started with the pigs. My research suggested this was the way to go, so I found myself some land near Cape Town and bought a herd. Willow Piggeries was under way and all went well. I loved the exercise of breeding animals, watching the sows producing and looking after their piglets. I have always enjoyed the thrill of birth, whatever the animal, and always regretted that I wasn't present at my children's births. In those days, it was not the done thing, and fathers were considered a nuisance in the delivery ward.

The main problem was always the cost of feed because a voracious herd of pigs seemed to do nothing all day apart from eat, eat and eat. I searched around for a solution, and luckily fell into conversation with the manager of a nearby supermarket, who happened to mention he was having trouble with disposing of the wastage, getting rid of milk, cheese, yoghurts, cakes, bread and anything else that was perishable.

A perfect deal was done: I solved his problem, and he solved mine.

My pig business was thriving and everybody seemed happy... except some of the neighbours because, soon after arriving in the area with my pigs, I had to start spreading the manure on the land and, if the wind happened to be blowing in the wrong direction, the smell was not the most fragrant.

One particular neighbour, Innes Droomer, was exceptionally upset, and, unfortunately, he decided to take his complaints to the police, and even the newspapers. All this furore must have inspired me to write a poem, which I recently discovered among my papers.

The Pig Pong Battle

It isn't just rumour
That one Innes Droomer
Objects to the pong of a pig
He phones up the papers
Does all sorts of capers
And generally acts like a prig.

Is it Laubscher or Schroeder
Who says that the odour
Is more than his volkies can stand
That no number of beatings
Short pay and ill-treatings
Will force them to stay on his land

When the South Easter blows
He puts hankie to nose
And hurries inside pretty quick
He shuts windows and doors
Cause the smell of the boars
Makes his visitors utterly sick

Brother Ed, you're in trouble
Come home at the double
Your name in the dirt's being flung
Your neighbours are rotten
So 't must not be forgotten
That the smell is not only pig dung.

That saga was a hassle, but some of my friends regarded the surplus of pig manure as an opportunity, and Peter Swart, my Western Province teammate, decided to take two big bags of the stuff to upgrade his vegetable garden.

We went round to his place the following week, and saw that he had dug a large trench where he had planted what he always referred to as his 'toms'. I must confess there was a strong and all too familiar smell around the place, but Swartie kept saying: "Don't worry about that. Wait till you taste my toms."

Eventually we were invited to a braai and the long-awaited 'tom-tasting' ceremony. The tomatoes looked fantastic, growing well, huge globes of scarlet, succulent and appealing. With great excitement, Swartie took the toms off the plants and went into the kitchen where his then girl-friend, a lady who he called Ginger Balls, was preparing the salad. She cut into the first tomato and, horror of horrors, found absolutely nothing inside.

Swartie was mortified and began cutting the others open. Every one was the same. Pig manure, we had all discovered, was so strong that it had to be used in very small quantities or this sort of thing happened. Peter could hardly console himself.

Well, the occasional whiff aside, the business did well and the factory seemed very happy with the quality we were producing, but then there was a glut and the nit-picking began. All our products sold were first grade, but very often I had to be content with second or third grade prices. I asked the retailers why they only gave me second grade status when I had never seen 'second grade' pork on sale in the shops. There was no reply. Perhaps the real problem was that I was an *'Engelsman'* in an industry dominated by Afrikaners.

It was never easy, but Helen did a fantastic job keeping things going while I was in Australia, playing World Series Cricket. In 1979 we found another 10 hectares of land to build more fattening and breeding pens.

One of my hobbies in those days was photography, and I bought myself a decent camera. We did have a couple of guns on the farm, which we used to shoot a snake now and then, or maybe just a guinea fowl for the pot, but I took much greater pleasure from shooting photographs rather than bullets. We had some great trips as a family, with Helen, Craig and Susan, and I still have vivid memories of that time.

Etosha Pan in Namibia was always a favourite because the massive saltpans are so spectacular. There was a small road which would take you right out onto the pan. Lion were hard to see but the giant herds of zebra, wildebeest and gemsbok were simply breathtaking as they meandered and frolicked across the plain. At the end of long, happy days driving around the park, we would take a drink down to the waterhole, find a seat, sit back, relax and watch the evening parade of animals wandering down to slake their thirst.

Back at Willow, we received a visit from an Extension Officer. These were officials appointed to assist land-owning farmers to advise them of any opportunities in the offing. Our officer arrived with the news that a beautiful Karoo farm of 36,000 hectares, just up the road, ideal for sheep farming, had become available. I knew that amount of land could only be managed by someone with more experience than I had but, with the officer's help, I decided to throw caution to the wind, and bought the place.

There was no doubt about its potential and, a week after completing the purchase, I stumbled upon someone who would prove an unlikely ally and friend. His name, he said was 'Oom Dick'. ('Oom' literally means uncle, but it is a form of address commonly used in Afrikaans-speaking communities as a term of respect for someone older). I first caught sight of him on the farm walking along a path towards me. He didn't look at all well and, in between coughing and sneezing, he told me he had been out looking for the ewes and their lambs, which he thought were being born.

"Well, can I help," I asked.

Oom Dick coughed and spluttered some more.

"I think you need some *muti* (medicine)," I said.

He was a small, wiry, middle-aged man wearing khaki shirt, trousers, thick socks and *veldskoene* (bush shoes), but I just picked him up, slung him over my shoulder, and carried him to his hut. We gave him a meal and he perked up, telling me how he could never thank me enough. Oom Dick and I soon became firm friends, and he turned out to be a mine of local information. I never tired of hearing his stories about the characters in the neighbourhood, nor even the more mysterious tales of death, ghosts and unexplained sightings that he loved to regale us with.

Our first task was to ensure the farm was properly fenced, repairing whatever was there and creating a new fence where there was nothing. Oom Dick proved a master of this trade and, having recruited a couple of his mates from the nearby town of Touwsriver, we all formed a fencing team, and set to work.

It wouldn't have been much fun wielding a ten-pound hammer and carrying rolls of wire fencing in the withering heat of a Karoo summer's day, but this was winter and, when we set out early in the morning, it was freezing. The wind whistled around us, chilling us to the bone. Nonetheless, we stuck to the task and made good progress.

To assist Oom Dick and his friends put up the fencing felt like joining a conductor and his orchestra. That might sound fanciful, but every time they rolled out a length of wire, Oom Dick would pull it tight, and then twang it. The sound would reverberate all the way down the line, getting fainter and fainter. Only when he was happy the noise was correct, and the tension was perfect, would he let his mate use the hammer and pin the wire to the posts.

As soon as the fencing was complete, we bought a truckload of sheep and a ram, and we were in business. Over the weeks and months that followed, I learned a major lesson about sheep farming. Actually producing the lambs is not too difficult. The hard part is getting them to market and selling them.

The buyers always found something wrong. The lambs were always 'too thin', or had 'something wrong with an eye', or couldn't 'walk straight', or the wool was 'too dirty and stringy'. They looked for any blemish to get the price down. It was intensely frustrating and, before too long, we decided to sell the place. The Karoo farm had proved too far from Willow Piggeries – 'just up the road' can be more than an hour's drive in this wide-open part of the world – and we really could not give the sheep the attention they needed. It was a pity, but we didn't do too badly out of the sale.

My marriage to Helen very sadly ended not long afterwards, and, with feed costs escalating and the price of pork fluctuating, eventually the pig farm was sold.

With my second wife, Julianne Bailey, we decided to make a brand new start, in the wonderful world of wine farming. Julianne found a farm called 'Bodega' in the district of Joostenbergvlakte, 40 kilometres from Cape Town. It was ideal: a Spanish-style house, two cottages, staff housing and outbuildings.

To be honest, I didn't know much about wine beyond how to drink it, so I asked an old mate and wine expert, Jan 'Boland' Coetzee, the former Springbok rugby player, to come and have a look before we bought the place. We had been told the vines produced 'Chenin Blanc' grapes, but Boland took one look and, in his inimitable way, declared: "*Dis nie Steen nie, dis ****** Cabernet.*'

We settled quickly. The name of the farm, Bodega, originated from the Spanish word for wine cellar, and that would cause us a few problems when we started to sell and market the wine, but it was a very beautiful place. The farm sat on a slight hill, offering a wonderful view of Table Mountain, and it was full of eucalyptus trees, which made good fodder for the small herd of cattle we bought to keep the place trim.

The two cottages, named Strawberry and Shepherd, were a real asset. We rented out one and prepared the other as a home for my parents. Gran and Pops proved a tremendous help on the farm, particularly in keeping things ticking over when I had to be away, coaching county cricket in England.

Dad had not been well for some time, and he died in 1992 following heart failure and respiratory problems. Both my parents were smokers; as a child, I used to dread the household chore of cleaning fag ends from whatever came to hand. The combination of those memories and seeing him become ill confirmed my strong opposition to smoking. I simply could not understand why people would want to do something that would, in all probability, kill them.

Still, the vines produced the grapes and, with a little luck and the invaluable help of Eugene and Gerda van Zyl, two wine experts we met by chance, we bought the cellar equipment and turned the grapes into some very decent wine. I still remember the great sense of achievement and pleasure on the day that our first vintage was declared ready to be put into oak barrels, where it would stay until the mobile bottling company arrived.

This first vintage turned out to be an absolute winner, and we ended up with double gold awards at the Young Wine Show. There was interest in our wine from Florida, in the USA, and, before long, case after case of wine was leaving the farm.

We took on a manager, planted some Pinotage and Merlot as well, and our vineyard was flourishing.

However, I still had my commitments as a cricket coach and, sadly, my relationship with Julianne began to unravel. It was a great pity for all concerned because our young wine cellar was doing so well but, in the end, we decided to go our separate ways. It was not an easy period of my life, to say the very least.

While I was coaching Gloucestershire in 1991, I had the good fortune to meet Cally Carroll during the Cheltenham festival. We got along famously and, again, together with Cally, I found myself looking for a new property to make a fresh start. There was no doubt in my mind that I wanted another vineyard and, while Cally was in England, I started the search.

Armed with some property brochures and an indomitable spirit, I headed off into the Boland to look at four properties, all of which sounded as though they might be interesting.

The first had a very grand Cape Dutch house, but the farm had no income because the owner had grubbed out all the vines. The second didn't have much land, and the third was an extraordinary house made from polystyrene bricks, but it was tucked away in the middle of a forest and probably too isolated

I seemed to have drawn a blank, but there was still one other farm to visit. I headed out towards the district of Robertson, through the Du

Toit's Kloof tunnel and on into the open lands of the Klein Karoo. It always amazes me how the terrain changed from one side of the mountains to the other. The Cape is so green and lush, but the other side is mostly scrub. Both areas, I should add, have wonderful grape-growing soil. The pass through to the tunnel was quite spectacular with huge mountains, their peaks soaring into the sky. Every winter, those peaks would send thunderous falls of white water crashing down to the river below.

Climbing up from the town of Robertson, I crested a hill and there, suddenly spread out before me was the beautiful valley, which, as I would later learn, is known locally as *Poespas Vallei*. I drove off the tarred road just before the cellar of Agterkliphoogte and finally arrived at the property called Spes Bona, a typically Afrikaans farm name albeit with a Latin origin.

It was, the owners told me, the second oldest house in the valley, but the curtains were drawn to keep out the sun and, understandably, it didn't seem in pristine condition. The farm was small by South African standards, measuring 189 hectares, mainly scrub but including fifteen hectares of vineyards, producing Chenin Blanc and Raisin Blanc grapes and a small stand of Colombard, the varieties that seemed to do well in this particular valley.

I looked around, and somehow it felt right. My next task was to persuade Cally that this was the place where we would be able to build our future together, and I felt sure she would share my vision. I picked her up from the airport and, just for the sake of providing some context, I thought it would be a good plan to start by showing her the first three houses.

She liked the look of the Cape Dutch house and, at one point, I sensed she had already started to decorate it in her mind. The other two were clearly too small and, on a perfect, beautiful Cape day, we made our way out, 30 kilometres outside Robertson.

Spes Bona was looking fantastic and, although the state of the house didn't win too many points, it was the amazing view from the highest point of the farm that clinched the deal. Mountains surrounded us on three sides.

After much of the unavoidable coming and going, waiting for papers to be signed, waiting for money to be deposited in the bank, we eventually concluded all the arrangements, and this special place in this special country was ours.

"One thing, Cally," the previous owners said, as they handed over the keys. "You will have to learn to speak Afrikaans, because nobody in this village speaks very much English."

"No problem," Cally replied, totally unfazed. "I'll speak English on Monday, Wednesday and Friday, then I'll speak Afrikaans on Tuesday and Thursday and, at weekends, I'll do whatever I feel like."

Word obviously spread through the local community because, just a week later, she went down to the local co-op winery at Agterkliphoogte on Tuesday morning and started to speak English to the wine maker Helmard Hannekom.

"*Nee, Cally*," he interrupted, with a broad grin across his face. "*Vandag is Dinsdag, en ek verstaan dis een van jou Afrikaanse dae.*"

We set to work. The white grape vines that we inherited were planted on the flat land around the house, but Cally and I decided our priority would be to produce our own red wine. We took advice from winemakers at the KWV and Elsenberg College, and decided to plant Pinotage, Merlot and Ruby Cabernet. This last grape was my personal favourite – I had tasted 'Ruby Cab' before and, even though it was used mainly for blending at that time, I thought it had real potential to become the red quaffing wine of the future.

I then took our *bakkie* up the mountain to look for a place to create our new red vineyard, and I found a spot that seemed ideal. Soil samples were taken, and the results were promising. So, with our four staff members, a huge yellow earthmover and the help of our neighbours, we prepared the ground. Poles and wire were ordered, and we bought the vines. The staff dug them in, and we watched with pride as our first red vineyard took shape before our eyes. In three years, it would be producing our first grapes.

It emerged that everybody in our district sent their grapes to the Agterkliphoogte Co-operative Cellar, and we happily sent our white grapes. There I spoke to the wine maker, however, and advised him that when our red grapes came on stream, we would be making our own red wine. He seemed fine with that, but I did sense a local curiosity about our plans. Growers in this area tended to produce 30 tonnes of grapes per hectare and, when we told people our red grapes would be restricted to nine tonnes per hectare, they fell about laughing.

"We want quality, not quantity," I said.

"You'll never make money," they replied.

Time would tell.

We had decided to rename the farm 'Windfall', and the place was looking lovely. The vineyard's prospects were excellent, but, boy, did it eat money! When we needed to finance the planting of some more vines, the bank manager was not too keen, but, yet again, cricket came up trumps. I was asked to coach Griqualand West, and that provided the funds for us to buy more vines and kit out the cellar with second-hand equipment. We were ready to make our own wine.

My cricket coaching did, however, prove a double-edged sword. On the one hand, it funded the development of Windfall but, on the other hand, it meant that I was away from the farm for long periods of time, and this forced us to employ a full-time manager to look after the place in my absence.

Initially all went well, and I vividly recall the great day when our first harvest of red grapes was ready. The staff were out picking the grapes. Cally was driving the *bakkie*, bringing the grapes from the vineyard to the cellar, where I was busy making sure the right amounts of chemicals went into the juice.

We were a happy team, working well together. When the pipes got bunged up with pips, we took the sieves from the kitchen and put them over the outlet pipe. That worked neatly and, before long, all that lovely juice was safe and sound in the tanks, and the cooling system set to work. I had hoped to bottle our own wine and complete the process ourselves, but that was beyond our means, and we sold it off as bulk.

Meanwhile, life in our valley was beginning to hot up.

The Directorate of the Co-op at Agterkliphoogte had initially appeared completely unconcerned by our plans to produce our own wine rather than send our grapes to them but, when we actually started, all hell let loose, and they threatened to take us to court. We were obviously ruffling some local feathers and, just when we sat down to plan our response, I was invited to move to Bangladesh and coach their national team.

Again, cricket offered funding and an exciting opportunity, which was great, but it was going to take us away from the farm, which was not great. We started to search for a farm manager who would keep things going while we were away and, if we had been able to find the right person, all would have been well.

Instead, through a combination of sheer bad luck and, I suppose, some bad judgement, we ended up being associated with a series of individuals who variously stole, swindled and lied. Susan, my daughter, did her best to help out, but poor old Windfall lurched from one crisis to another.

We did find some diamonds among what became a terrible, depressing situation, like Pauli Viljoen, who worked like Trojan, but he had to leave after just nine months. That was typical.

In the end, I phoned the ex-cricketer Lawrence Seeff, and told him we wanted to auction the farm. He put us in touch with someone called Andy Todd, from an auction house.

"Don't worry," he said. "Let me do the worrying."

After everything that had happened, it was just a relief to hear somebody say those words. The farm was sold and Cally and I accepted so very, very sadly that our Windfall dream would not come true.

Chapter Thirteen – Political Days

I always loathed the policy of apartheid. I loathed the concept of people being classified by their race or the colour of their skin. I loathed legislative discrimination against people because of their race.

I loathed the Population Registration Act, which allocated every South African into one or other racial group. In order of preference, these were whites, Indians, coloureds and blacks. Intermarriage between these groups was strictly forbidden. If it did take place, the persons concerned could apply to have his or her racial status changed, not upwards but downwards. So, if a designated coloured person married a black person, the coloured person would become officially registered as black.

The Nationalist Party, the architects of this insane racial engineering, were acting like God, and the madness knew no bounds. Officials used all kinds of tests to determine a person's race: if a pencil was stuck into hair and the hair curled around the pencil, the person was not white; if the whites of the eyes were slightly brownish rather than white, the person was not white; if moons on the fingernails were bluish rather than white, the person could not be white. Such lunacy took place in South African government offices day after day.

If a white man was driving somewhere with his coloured or black housemaid, she would have to sit in the back or it would be assumed that they were having a relationship; and if this was proven to be the case – and the police had extraordinary powers – each participant would typically spend six months in jail.

I also loathed the Group Areas Act, which compelled each racial group to live in its own area. The ruthless implementation of this law resulted in entire communities being uprooted and moved elsewhere, simply because the place where they had lived for generations was now designated as a white area.

The government's brutality is hard to conceive. Bulldozers would simply arrive, and reduce established black or coloured communities to rubble. Most infamously, District Six, a coloured area near the Cape Town city centre, was flattened, and the inhabitants moved 12 miles away to Mitchell's Plain, but this same cruelty was meted out to black and coloured South Africans the length and breadth of the country.

It sometimes got even worse. In Johannesburg, once the bustling, black community in Sophiatown had been forcibly removed, the government named the new white suburb 'Triomf' (Triumph).

I loathed these laws, and I loathed apartheid, but I never had the honour of being thrown into prison for my beliefs, partly because I didn't do anything too serious to draw attention to myself, partly because, as a relatively high-profile white sportsman, the 'Nats' preferred to harass, but tolerate, me.

Should I have done more?

Perhaps. I don't know. Maybe I wasn't brave enough, but I didn't believe in the armed struggle and reached the conclusion that I could achieve more to undermine the system inside South Africa and out of jail, than I could ever have achieved either in exile or in jail.

Looking back, a liberal outlook was instilled in me from an early age. There was never any discrimination either at WHPS, my primary school, or at Pretoria Boys High School. I was eager to enrol at Wits University, which was renowned in those days as a hotbed of liberalism. The Government often referred to Wits students as 'communists', but that didn't bother us because we knew that anybody who opposed apartheid was called a communist.

I involved myself in the student body, and remember many evenings spent with friends, secretly at their homes, listening as they related firsthand experiences of the government's brutality in the townships. Some of these people were repeatedly intimidated and detained without trial. One of my lecturers at Wits was Robert Sobukwe, who became leader of the banned Pan-African Congress. These were hectic times.

We organised many demonstrations with anti-apartheid placards, and the police would usually arrive, charging at us with guns and batons. On one occasion they were particularly violent, smashing all the placards and taking whichever students they could catch to the Fort, a prison in Johannesburg.

The rest of us decided we would march on the Fort and demand the release of our friends. After preparing a new set of placards, about 200 of us arrived in the street outside the prison.

"Set them free," we chanted. "Set them free! Set them free!"

The Fort had been designed exactly like a fort, and it wasn't long before we saw security policemen peering out from between the castellated battements on the roof.

"Disperse within three minutes," boomed a policeman with a loud hailer, "Or we will fire on you."

We chanted even louder.

"Disperse within two minutes," the voice over the loud hailer came again, "Or we will fire on you."

More men appeared on the roof, and we saw they were armed with guns capable of spraying the street with a devastating volley of bullets. This was not a game. I remember looking at my friends, their faces were contorted with rage, and they were still chanting. It felt as if we were facing a firing squad.

"Set them free!"

"Set them free!"

"Set them free!"

"Disperse within one minute, or we will fire on you."

Nobody wanted to become a statistic, lying dead on the pavement so, almost as one, we turned and legged it through the streets of Hillbrow. Even then, as we ran, none of us could be sure we would not receive a bullet in the back. This was the crazy reality of South Africa in the early 1960s and, because of severe press censorship and living in segregated cocoons, most white people had no idea what was happening. Newspapers would often appear with various words or articles blacked out.

Many of my fellow students decided to leave the country, and some of them, like Aziz Pahad, would return to play a major role as ANC government ministers. I remember considering my own situation at Wits and deciding to become an early member of the Progressive Federal Party

(PFP), a political party started by Dr Jan Steytler and Colin Eglin with the unequivocal aim of abolishing apartheid.

As my cricket career developed, I continued to take an active interest in politics but, in truth, I never raised my head above the parapet. For me at that time, sport became my absolute priority.

Even so, I kept my eyes wide open. While we were living in Port Elizabeth, Helen was helped during the birth of our son, Craig, by a doctor called Gavin Blackburn. His wife Molly was a wonderful woman, who made herself available to assist the black community at all times of the day and night. One morning, we heard that Molly and a friend had been killed in a 'car accident', although foul play was suspected.

Her death prompted a huge outpouring of grief, and buses ferried mourners from the local townships to the funeral. Many of these people were carrying wooden guns and wearing ANC colours.

The security forces arrived and parked their vast, eight-wheeled *ratels* (troop carriers) to form a ring of steel around the church. As the highly charged, emotional service came to a conclusion, there was a deafening barrage of noise outside. It was, as we later discovered, caused by soldiers beating their batons against the sides of the ratels. That might sound insignificant, but it was extremely frightening. There was terror, real terror, in the eyes of the people sitting around us inside that church, and we were relieved to get home safely.

Still, even though cricket remained uppermost in my mind, during the late 1960s and 1970s, the indefensible idiocy of apartheid started to infringe on the sporting side of my life. My hatred of the Nats and their policies intensified during the D'Oliveira affair, and our consequent isolation from international cricket.

The sheer pettiness of government policy was felt even at provincial level. The Western Province team was returning from an away match by coach when we stopped to have a beer at a pub in Somerset West. Omar Henry, the gifted spin bowler, was a member of our side, but I didn't envisage a problem.

"Hey, he can't come in," said the bartender, pointing at Omar, who was classified as coloured.

I protested.

"Just call this number in Pretoria," the bartender said. "It's a 24-hour number and you should be able to get a special dispensation for your friend to have a beer in here as well."

I duly dialled the number, and Omar had his beer. This ridiculous procedure happened several times and we complied, but, on one occasion when Omar was bluntly barred from entering a steakhouse, the rest of us stood up and left in protest. We vowed never to return to the restaurant, and we never did.

Through these cricketing years I maintained my membership of the PFP, but I only started to play an active role when I worked within Dr Frederik van Zyl Slabbert's campaign to be elected as MP for Rondebosch, in Cape Town. Van Zyl Slabbert later became leader of the PFP, and a man who inspired those around him. He was a fine politician and a brilliant speaker, whose intelligence was matched by his integrity. The Rondebosch constituency was close to Newlands, and I was happy to help, phoning around, getting out the voters.

Another time, I assisted the party by donating a pig to their fund-raising fete. This involved transporting the porker, already slaughtered and chilled, but still in one piece, from my Willow Piggery farm into Cape Town. I tried a few methods, but it seemed the only way I could do this was to prop the animal up in the passenger seat of the car while I drove. This unusual spectacle startled other motorists, and there was a repeat performance later in the day when I was asked to take the pig home and cut it into smaller pieces.

Perhaps naively, I was starting to believe the tide was turning against apartheid and, perhaps, South Africa would be able to move forward. I was making no secret of my views, and the PFP seemed to be making progress. One day in 1980, I received a telephone call at home from Van Zyl Slabbert. He explained how John Wiley, the United Party MP for Simonstown, had crossed the floor to the Nats and precipitated a by-election. He asked me whether I would be willing to stand as the PFP candidate. This was a huge honour for me and, as my cricket career was nearing its conclusion, I eagerly agreed.

A selection process was held, and I just about stumbled through some aggressive questioning by people who wondered whether a cricketer could survive in the political world. I was eventually confirmed as the PFP candidate to take on John Wiley, who had held the Simonstown seat since 1966.

Some of my mates warned me that politics was a cut-throat business, where dog eats dog, and they were right. In those days, the Nats liked to invite representatives of other parties to their meetings, and then to try to humiliate them. I went along to one particular NP meeting in Paarl, and spoke on 'Politics in Sport – How to Solve the Problem'. My argument was essentially that apartheid had put politics into sport and the simple solution was to get rid of it. There followed an intense, hostile debate about our country's future.

Each time I spoke, I noticed that a man standing at the back of the hall would scribble down what I had said. He obviously wasn't a journalist, and it seemed as if he was a member of the security forces, checking on me. Towards the end of the meeting, this sinister individual suddenly got up to leave.

"Oh no, please don't leave," I shouted after him, cheekily. "I have much more to say."

My remark didn't go down well with the audience, and people came up to me afterwards telling me that the government had such a difficult job to do that I shouldn't be so hard on them. I was amazed how they could be so blind to the evil of apartheid. At any rate, I grew accustomed to the fact that every time I spoke, there would be a mystery man standing at the back of the venue, noting down everything I said. Eventually I began to take transcripts of my speeches to the meetings and, as soon as I saw one of these men get out his pad and pencil, I would approach them and say: "Oh please don't bother trying to keep up with me. Here is a copy of what I am going to say."

I started the Simonstown campaign confident that we would win, and fully expecting that I would become an MP, but politics is about much more than being convinced of your own position. The NP mounted an effective campaign to instil fear into the voters and Wiley fought hard.

I found myself being asked about ridiculous rumours that Harry Oppenheimer, a known PFP sympathiser, had helped me buy some land in the area. The political sledging was quite heavy: they lampooned my background in cricket, calling me Barlow, PFP – Played for Province.

I was living under a microscope and, to be honest, I didn't enjoy the experience at all. I remember telling a friend that I would rather face the world's fastest bowler from 22 yards, than John Wiley in a by-election.

However, I was not the type to back down, and I struggled on. Many people worked tirelessly for my cause, and I was very touched by their commitment. It was humbling for me to see so many good South Africans giving so much of their time to create a country of which we could all feel proud.

We canvassed street after street, from house to house and, at one point, a lady asked me directly: "Would you allow coloured people to move in next door to me?"

"Yes," I replied, without hesitation.

"I don't like coloured people," the lady said. "They're not clean."

Just at that moment, there was a terrible noise as a motorbike revved up. I peaked over the fence, and saw a bunch of typical Hell's Angels, with filthy clothes, in the next house.

"That's awful," I remarked, sighing, "but you can't pick your neighbours, you know."

My outstanding memory of the by-election was the opportunity to speak on the same platform as Helen Suzman, a hero of the anti-apartheid movement, at a public meeting in Muizenberg.

A few minutes before we were due to start, I was called to the phone at a public telephone box close to the stage. This was odd, but I picked up the receiver and said hello.

"Hello, Eddie Barlow," a strange voice replied. "We have put a bomb under the platform, and it is going to explode in around 10 minutes. We don't want you, but we want Suzman."

Then, the line went dead. My first reaction was to panic. I rushed to tell Mrs Suzman what had happened, suggesting that we should cancel the meeting and leave immediately.

I will never forget what happened next. She held me firmly by the arm, and said: "Don't worry. I have had hundreds of those calls. Nothing will happen. We will start at 7.00 pm, as planned."

The grand old lady of South African politics dragged me back to the stage and, before long, we noticed the presence of some strange men in white overalls with sniffer dogs. The police had taken the threat seriously, but their search of the entire area revealed nothing. As they left, Mrs Suzman leaned across and, with a gentle smile, whispered in my year: "I told you so. They just threaten. They are cowards."

Helen Suzman was the bravest woman I ever met. She never flinched in the face of the Nats, and emerged as nothing less than a truly great South African. With her, the party leaders, Colin Eglin, Van Zyl Slabbert and Alex Boraine, transformed the PFP from a pretty ordinary bunch into a vibrant official opposition party. Unfortunately, much to my disappointment, I was not able to join them as an MP in parliament.

After all the handshaking and speechmaking, the outcome of the Simonstown by-election was announced, and it transpired Wiley had defeated me by 1,185 votes. It was close, but not close enough. I believed too many English-speaking voters who had indicated their intention to vote for me had been scared back to support the Nats. I was disappointed, but determined to continue the fight in whatever capacity was possible.

In 1984 I was asked to open a South African Sports Office in London. The idea was to create a pro-active body, funded by South African sports federations and independent from government, which would be able to put the case for South African sport to the wider international community.

My brief was to inform decision-makers and the media about the huge steps being taken by South African sports bodies towards the elimination of racial discrimination in sport, and, in effect, to counter the activities of Sam Ramsamy, who was running SANROC (the South African Non-Racial Olympic Committee) and arguing there for total isolation, saying their could be no normal sport in an abnormal society.

We started by commissioning research, which showed that 90 per cent of British people supported sports contact with South Africa as a means of encouraging the pace of wider reform. I believed international recognition of progress in SA sport would persuade the government to abandon the policy of apartheid. Looking back, I am not sure that I was right, but I'm also not sure I was completely wrong either.

Most of the British media took an opposite view and, from the outset, I knew we faced an uphill struggle to make any progress. With a modest budget we worked hard to lobby MPs, journalists, sports administrators and businessmen, and, before long, we published our 'Declaration of Intent'.

This document confirmed our commitment to abolish racist legislation and create equal opportunities for all South African sportsmen and women, and it outlined a strategy whereby each SA sports federation would develop its own programme to ensure these goals were achieved within their own structures.

The response was generally positive and over the course of the next three years I continued to argue the case for engagement rather than isolation. Life was never dull. Sometimes my speeches would be disrupted, several times I was spat upon, quite a few times I would have to be bundled away through the back door; at other times I would score a few points.

I also befriended many interesting people like novelist Jeffrey Archer, journalist Ian Wooldridge, politician John Carlisle and former rugby player John Taylor. They didn't always agree with me, but we got along. Some days Denis Thatcher would come to the SA Sports office at 150 Regent Street for a large gin-and-tonic and a chat about the situation. I think he relayed our conversations to his wife, the Prime Minister, who wanted to be kept informed of what was going on.

After a few months in London I reckoned it was important for me to have a meeting with the South African government.

My idea was that I would report what I had discovered in London, specifically that the government should encourage multi-racial sport as the precursor for wider reform. Van Zyl Slabbert arranged a meeting for me with State President PW Botha, and I duly arrived at the Union Buildings in Pretoria.

Botha was nicknamed the *Groot Krokodil* (Great Crocodile) because he could be so snappy. As I tried to outline my proposal, I sensed I was about to have some personal experience of his nature. He started by saying how difficult it was to be President, and how everybody demanded change. However, I continued to put my case and I sensed he was starting to boil, becoming more and more angry.

Suddenly, the door of the State President's office flew open, and the young naval officer who had shown me in appeared. He appeared to be concerned and looked directly at me.

I asked: "What's the problem?"

"Are you all right," he asked, looking at me.

"I'm fine."

It later transpired that it was this guy's job to interrupt meetings when the discussion became too heated and, sure enough, that turned out to be the end of our meeting, and I was ushered away. At least, I had managed to make my point, but I was not overly optimistic that PW would do anything about it.

I returned to London, to the cycle of press conferences, lobbying and private meetings, mixing with people like Trevor Huddlestone and Peter Hain, a prominent anti-apartheid campaigner who went to my old school, Pretoria Boys High, and is now a Cabinet Minister in the UK.

Everything seemed to boil down to a battle of two slogans: the 'no normal sport in an abnormal society' being pedalled by SANROC and Sam Ramsamy, against our 'equal opportunities through sport'. Maybe I was being too idealistic, but I really believed isolation had served its purpose, and that it was time to engage SA sport.

The months passed, and, beyond the SA Sports Office, Helen and I enjoyed living in Richmond, where I had bought a small cruiser called *Nikki Nimbi* and spent many happy hours on the River Thames. By 1987, however, I began to realise we had taken the argument just about as far as it would go. I decided that the most effective way to bring about real change in South Africa would be to return home and work at grass roots level.

Some people said I had wasted my time in London, and there were times when, privately, I might well have agreed with them. We did make progress at various stages on various levels but, no matter the rights and wrongs of the argument, the simple reality was that, whatever the individual South African sports federations might have done to encourage multi-racial competition and end discrimination, South Africa would continue to be isolated and punished so long as the evil apartheid laws remained on the statute books.

In the last days of my spell in London, becoming increasingly frustrated by what I regarded as lack of momentum for change, I sat down with Morgan Davies and Robyn Owen, two friends who usually helped me prepare my presentations, and developed plans to launch a new organisation which, on reflection, was maybe a few years ahead of its time.

SANSA, which stood for Sporting Action in the New South Africa, produced a manifesto under the giant headline *APARTHEID SUCKS...* and, in smaller letters: *the lifeblood out of SA sport.*

I recently came across this document in my files. It is dated 1987, but has never been published. Here are a few excerpts:

I've had enough. And I am going to do something about it. So are you. What can we do to change our country? That's the question that's been put to me by thousands of South Africans, black and white. I tell them what we can do. Not because I'm clever, but because I spend my life listening, reading, talking, and hearing what people want. We agree that South Africa must change. We agree with each other. But nothing happens. We don't do anything about it. Well, I've had enough. Now I'm going to do something about it.

I've spent the past three years working my butt off in London, representing South African sport. I've been in more television studios than the South African Ambassador and all his staff put together. I've been in more Parliamentary offices and more business offices and more newspaper offices than any other South African during that time. I know how the world sees South Africa. I know why it sees us like that. No, it is not just that the world doesn't understand us. It's not just that the world is ignorant about us. It's got a lot to do with the fact that we haven't done nearly enough to create a fair society in South Africa.

What am I going to do? I'm going to get you to help me change this country. **We are South Africa**. *You and me. All of us...*

We all know what we want – a democracy that offers equal opportunities to all. But we are being bluffed. It's the politicians who tell us that we, the ordinary people, must leave it to them. We can't change our society. Well, they're wrong. Society can change itself. We can force the politicians to accept the changes we want... It is our politicians – white and black – who have made us the world's polecat...

I've come back to South Africa several times a year while I've been based in London and each time more and more people say: "Eddie, we're going down the tube, the whole damn country. They'll never change." 'They' means Pretoria. And more and more people have said to me: "Eddie, we just can't win. They'll never understand us or accept us, whatever we do." 'They' means the rest of the world. Now people tell me: "Eddie, it's hopeless. Whatever we do, they'll never be satisfied. They want the lot." 'They' means the ANC.

What nonsense is this? We can change the country if we decide to and if we put enough effort and energy into it. I've had meeting after meeting with government leaders, top politicians and business people. I doubt that more than a few South Africans have had meetings with more Cabinet Ministers during the course of their work than I've had. And I can tell you that my gloomy friends are half-right. The politicians won't change. But I'm damned if I'm going to stand by and watch my country going down the tube. We have to change the politicians. I'm going to start – and you are going to help me.

I'm coming into the political arena, and so are you. We're going to change South Africa. We're not going to do so by becoming politicians ourselves, God forbid. Power is what we're talking about. Power is what we already have. Now we're going to use it. People Power, economic power.

Ignore the extremists on all sides. It's the many millions of good, decent South Africans in the middle, of all colours, who must accept the challenge to use their power to take over the country and send the politicians and civil servants packing, back where they belong.

So many people have tried to start the ball rolling, but it never keeps moving. Why not? Because we're all waiting for the other guy to pick it up and run with it. We're waiting for the other guy to compromise. We're waiting for Mandela to be released. Or we're waiting for people to be released from detention. Or we're waiting for the ANC to renounce violence. We're just pussyfooting around.

I've had enough. I'm going to do something about it.

I'm starting with you, business people and sports people. We're going to change South Africa. Believe me. And we start by making this declaration here and now, together...

We stand for abandoning the Group Areas Act and separate education. Not in ten years time, not next year. NOW. All forms of economic discrimination must be scrapped. Now. We must have a Bill of Rights that protects all South Africans and which is enforced by independent courts. Influx control must be abandoned...

As sportsmen and businessmen, we must promote contact. You must do so in your business, in your home and in your sports club. You must do so in your neighbourhood, in your local shopping centre and in your streets. You must stand up against racism and against discrimination.

I'm not asking you to support any political party. I'm asking you to stand up and support the concept of all South Africans living together, respecting each other's basic human rights.

That's all. It's as simple as that.

Do something! Contact me and my organisation. In six months time, or sooner, we're going to be in a position to tell the politicians who we represent and what we represent. And they'll be able to see for themselves just how powerful a group has come together to create and present an alternative for South Africa.

I've had enough and I'm going to do something about it. Now.

That was my clarion call, and it was circulated to a select group of prominent sports administrators, but they took fright at the bluntness of the message, and nothing happened. The late 1980s were a nervous time and, although the National Party had started to talk about reform, people tended to hesitate. They weren't ready for change and decisive action.

Some people didn't like my outspoken approach. My telephone was tapped, my post was opened and, at Bodega, we often had visits from the police in the middle of the night, harassing our staff, who happened to be receiving a decent living wage. The authorities didn't appreciate that either.

I didn't mind.

This was my clarion call.

It seemed as if nobody was listening.

Six years later, enough people listened to Nelson Mandela, and that made me the happiest man in the world.

Then, with the birth of the new South Africa, and the writing of a constitution that protected the rights of each and every South African, at last, we had a country of which we could feel justly proud.

Chapter Fourteen – Coaching Days

Talking about cricket, discussing the way the game should be played, analysing players' problems and developing solutions: such activities always seemed more like pleasure than work to me, so I suppose it was inevitable that, sooner or later, I should fall into some kind of coaching role.

I returned to South Africa after my stint at the SA Sports Office in London and worked for two years in the financial services sector. That was fine, but I missed the game and I was pleased to receive a phone call in 1990 from Frank Twistleton, the President of the Gloucestershire County Cricket Club. He said the team was struggling, and asked if I would return to England and help them put things right.

Frank put an exciting and generous contract on the table, and I signed on the dotted line. This would be my first coaching job, and it took me back into the game that I still loved so much.

I arrived to find the media having a field day because Gloucestershire had lost a few matches. They were all overreacting, but the situation was typical of professional sport. Administrators are generally quick to panic after a few bad results; then, somebody like me is summoned, and we are expected to be some kind of wizard who waves his magic wand and puts everything right. Of course, it's never so simple.

In my experience, the problem is almost always a lack of quality players; so my first message is that nobody should expect the team's fortunes to improve overnight because it takes time to identify talent, and a tremendous amount of work from everyone to bring it through to the level required.

An easy option is to blame the administrators, but that is not always helpful. Quality administrators need to learn their trade, just like players, and that isn't an instant process either.

I discovered Gloucestershire were suffering from both these syndromes, and the county also appeared to be unhealthily obsessed with a project to redevelop their ground, rather than the team. I tried to focus everybody on the cricket and, as ever, tried to build some degree of spirit among the squad.

One or two players were complaining about their salaries, wheeling out the age-old comparison with golfers and tennis players and declaring they were been exploited. The analogy with these individual sports is bogus, and cricketers simply have to accept they will be paid what the market can afford. Whether in England, South Africa or anywhere, the game derives its income from TV rights, sponsorship and gate receipts. When, and if, these happen to rise, then there is more for counties and provinces to spend on salaries.

It's that simple. Officials can't pay money they don't have. I tried to go through these issues, but it wasn't easy to make progress, and our task was further complicated when club officials constantly criticised the team. At one point, one senior office bearer at the club had the audacity to tell me: "You're wasting your time with these chaps, Eddie. You can't be expected to make a silk purse out of a sow's ear."

Well, it was my job to try.

We had an exceptionally talented all rounder in the team, but his mind was everywhere but on playing decent cricket. He approached me one day, declaring he could not bowl anymore, and he pushed some X-rays under my nose as 'proof'. Well, that meant absolutely nothing to me.

"Look," I replied. "You are contracted to bat and to bowl. If you're telling me you can't do half your job, then you should go and see the Club Secretary and he'll renegotiate your deal. OK?"

The player didn't like that. Eventually, we released him, which caused a rumpus with some of the members, but it was the right thing to do. Sometimes, you have to bite the bullet.

This was also the case with another senior player who was, to be blunt, partying too hard. I was aware of the problem and hoped the situation could be managed, but one day he turned up at the club after a long lunch, clearly the worse for wear. We had no option but to release him from his contract as well.

The cumulative effect of such unpleasant and irritating incidents was

My grandson Michael seems to be enjoying a visit to my favourite restaurant, La Petite Ferme in Franschhoek

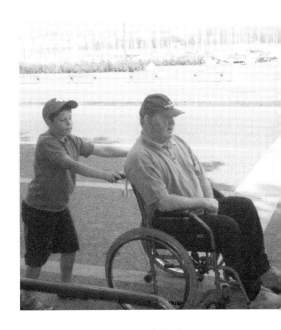

My grandson Henry manfully keeps me on the move during a holiday in Switzerland

My grandson Hamish joins me for a cuddle in my wheelchair

My grandson Ruaridh – my pal and right hand man – in Jersey, Christmas 2005

that I was tempted to adopt a new dictum: whenever you arrive to coach a new team, don't tamper with the senior players. That would have been the easy way, but it would not have helped the team. I had to do what I believed was right.

Slowly, working hard, goading and encouraging the guys, we started to develop a team around a group of talented cricketers, and I began to think we were making progress.

David 'Syd' Lawrence was a huge, strong man, and he emerged with every quality required for an international fast bowler. He practised diligently and started to pick up wickets on a regular basis. His reward was selection to play for England, and I was delighted that all his efforts had borne fruit.

Jack Russell was another of our players who was playing for England. He was a fine wicketkeeper and a born professional sportsman, who looked after himself very, very well and was continually focused on the job. Jack had several idiosyncrasies, some of which he developed in India: for example, he always kept a couple of tins of baked beans in his cricket bag. His·idea was that, if ever felt peckish, he would always have something at hand which he could be 100% certain was safe to eat. Well, it just became a habit. Some of the players teased him mercilessly, and, one day, his baked beans went missing. Jack was not at all happy.

Mark Alleyne was another delightful character who played his cricket with a smile on his face. If the ball was there to be hit, he hit it. An excellent fielder and a tidy medium-paced bowler, he moved swiftly up the ladder, was appointed to captain the England A side, and he later captained the county.

Our overseas professional was Courtney Walsh, the great West Indian fast bowler, who proved totally and utterly dedicated to his cricket. He set a fine example, and was a pleasure to have around. There is no doubt that overseas players, like Courtney and others, raised the standard of county cricket, but it would certainly serve the interests of the England team better if their number were to be gradually reduced.

There were other characters. Martyn Ball, our off-spinner, had started to see a beautiful Scandinavian girl called Mona, to whom he is now married. He got quite a ribbing about this, and I walked up to her one day and asked: "Do I detect a little Gloucestershire accent there, Mona?"

As she replied that she thought so, I asked her why that was. From somewhere behind me, there came the burr of Bally in his deepest vernacular: "Coz 'er lives with oi."

Andy Babington, one of our quickies, was the proud owner of two large Doberman-type dogs of unknown ancestry and one day I saw him taking one of them for a walk around the boundary.

"Hey, Andy, what's your dog called," I asked, casually.

"Deefer," he replied.

"Deefer? What kind of a name is that?"

"Dee for dog."

Gloucestershire played their home matches at several venues, mainly at the County Ground in Bristol, but also at a quaint ground in Moreton-in-Marsh. There were also a couple of annual festival weeks. The Gloucester Festival was played at the Wingate ground, then known as the Wagon Works, but it has since moved to the King's School. The prestigious Cheltenham Festival remains a major social event.

It was, in fact, at Cheltenham where I met Cally. I had been doing a little perambulation around the ground, as was my habit, and I noticed her sitting alone with her scorebook on her lap.

"What's the score?"

She told me, and, after a few pleasantries, off I walked.

The following day, I was standing outside the changing room near the gate as she arrived, late.

"What's this?" I asked, smiling. "The scorer can't arrive late!"

We started chatting. I offered her a coffee and the rest, as they say, is history.

My time at Gloucestershire was curtailed when my father fell ill, and it became necessary for me to return to South Africa. In truth, a parting of company seemed to be for the best, especially when the chairman of the cricket committee told me in no uncertain terms that he did not support my strategy for the team.

I returned to my duties on the farm... until the telephone rang yet again. It was the Free State Cricket Union, and they wanted me to coach their provincial team during the 1991/92 season.

It was obviously an exciting challenge and, well, I have rarely been able to resist a challenge, so I organised a manager at the farm and prepared to spend a lot of my time in Bloemfontein. This city is frequently perceived as dull and conservative but I have always enjoyed the place and its predominantly Afrikaans-speaking population. I spoke the *taal* (language), and found the people sincere and dedicated.

On my very first visit, I started work with the young Free State captain, a certain Hansie Cronjé.

Now the last thing I want this book to be is an exercise in blowing my own trumpet but I hope the following piece is enlightening. Cally asked me if I thought Hansie would write a piece for this book when it was first envisaged. She e-mailed him and this is what he sent back. The words are all his and they give his version of what happened when I arrived as the new Free State coach. I was touched by what he wrote, and phoned him to thank him for his words. That was the last time we spoke.

The Coach by Hansie Cronjé

It was 05h45 in Bloemfontein and the sun was barely up on a cool spring day, when the telephone rang at home. I struggled to the phone, still feeling the effects of a few beers the night before.

I mumbled: "Hello?"

"Wake up, you fool."

I was stunned.

"Wake up, captain. I was watching some cricket on TV last night and those Pakistanis sure know how to swing that ball. I need to meet you at the nets at 06h00. I have a plan."

Didn't this new coach know that students and cricketers sleep until ten in the morning? Imagine the surprise on my face when I arrived at the nets at 06h05 to find the former South African Test all-rounder covered from head toe in some kind of glue.

He saw my reaction, and explained: "I thought I may as well do something useful with my time in Bloem, so I am building a lekker little sailboat."

I wasn't sure why he had to do it at 05h00, but that was our man, Bunter Barlow.

"Strap them on, captain!"

I could barely see the nets through my sleepy eyes. The covers had been removed and they were beautifully mown, rolled and marked, yet there were no ground staff in sight at this time of the morning.

"This, young man, is my garden, my patch. It is my job to provide you with the best training facilities in the world, and I will make sure they are world class. Don't come piss in my patch!"

Here was a man who was proud of his little 'garden', not asking who will do it, not blaming others for not having done it but taking responsibility and making those nets the best in the west. They were still in the shade as the sun battled to get up over Naval Hill. I asked him whether he ever slept.

"Sleep?" he boomed. *"Sleep is what we do for the three or four hours when we are not working. There is a World Cup to be won in February next year, and I want four Free Staters in that squad."*

I felt like saying to the man, 'Hey, this is Bloem, my mate. This is not Jo'burg or Cape Town. We've only got Alan Donald here, and we haven't won a match yet', but I decided to keep quiet.

"Let's go, captain. Give me 60 shuttles before we start. You know what a shuttle is? It's a 25-metre sprint. Did you know that the average batsman hits 10 boundaries in every 100 runs that he scores? That means he has to run at least 60 of those runs. Now start running!"

When then was done, as I wandered wearily to start batting in the nets, I asked the coach if he would start the bowling machine at a gentle 50mph, just to get my eye in.

"Sure!" he replied, with a touch of venom.

The first ball came at me at 90mph, an inswinging yorker that hit me smack bang on the left foot. Believe me at 06h30, seven degrees Celsius, it's no fun getting hit on the toe by a cricket ball.

"Wake up, you fool! Watch the ball. Get your feet out of the way. Use your bat and tuck those elbows in! Come on! Let's see some discipline!"

Six months later, the flight from Jo'burg to Perth had three Free Staters *on board on the way to represent South Africa at the 1992 Cricket World Cup – Allan Donald, Omar Henry and myself. A fourth, Corrie van Zyl, was desperately unlucky not to make the team, but joined up with the squad for the Test series in the West Indies two months later. That was the quartet of Free Staters he wanted in the team.*

We had just won the Nissan Shield one-day competition, and finished runners-up in the four-day Castle Cup competition. It was partly my fault because, in a match against Eastern Province, I dropped Kepler Wessels on 4, and he went on to score 147 not out and win the match. If we had won, we'd have won the Castle Cup as well.

They say that transformational leaders all have a vision. Well, Eddie Barlow had a vision, for himself and for every team he played in or coached. He wanted to be the best and he believed he was.

Transformational leaders empower followers and motivate them to achieve that vision. Eddie did that. At the end of that season, a Free State team who had been the Cinderellas of SA cricket started to believe they were the best side in the country, and we won nine trophies in the following seven years.

Even though he only spent six months as Free State coach, his legacy lived on for many, many years after he left, and he deserves a lot of credit for our success during the 1990s.

As soon as he was appointed, some people warned me about Bunter, saying he was a good coach of young cricketers, because he could motivate them, but did not know how to handle any senior players. How wrong they were! He built that Free State side around four experienced all-rounders: Franklyn Stephenson, who was 34 years old, Corrie van Zyl, who was 31, Omar Henry, 37, and Brad Player, 30.

All of these players had scored at least one century by the end of the season, each of them was bowling superbly, and they all had a magnificent attitude and great respect for the new coach. It's a fact no team managed to score more than 200 in any one-day match against us that season.

I remember Franklyn was late for the first practice. Eddie took the rest of the team and made us do fitness until Frankie arrived 45 minutes later. Needless to say, he never arrived late again. Another time, I finished a 4km fitness run some distance ahead of the back runners, and the coach made me turn around and fetch them, barking after me: "Because we're a team, captain, not just a bunch of individuals."

Eight years later, in 1998, after suffering the disappointment of losing the final two Test matches, and the series, on tour to England, South Africa were facing up to the West Indies for the first time in a full series at home. We hired Bunter again to assist the national team, and help us prepare for the onslaught.

"I am a strange bloke," he told the guys. "People will tell you this and that about the Windies. I will only say this to you: don't let them come and piss on our patch." The history books record that South Africa completed only the seventh whitewash ever in Test cricket history. Did he play a role? You bet he did.

Like so many of the greatest players and coaches all over the cricket world, Eddie based his success on two simple principles: discipline and fitness. As he always told me: "Captain, respect the game, Mother Cricket, and keep your own disciplines, and you'll be just fine."

That was Hansie's view, set down before his public downfall and his tragically early death. What can I say about this extraordinary individual whom I first met as the nine-year-old captain of a schoolboy team who turned up to what seemed a rather insignificant coaching course?

Well, the first thing is that he was blessed with extraordinary parents. Ewie, his father, was a very fine and popular Free State cricketer, who later became an excellent president of the union, and his mother San-Marie gave her three children, Hansie, Frans and Hester, every opportunity going.

Second, he was an exceptional captain. It is astonishing how leadership stands out so early in life. Hansie's knowledge of the game was wide and deep, and he was always willing to learn more. He was also a disciplinarian, who, if he wanted something done, would spell out his instructions and check to see if they had been followed. I have known many captains who avoided confrontation with their players because they lacked the confidence that what they were doing was correct. Hansie was certainly self-confident.

Third, as captain of the South African team from 1994 until his resignation in 2000, he earned the absolute respect of the leading cricketers in South Africa, and in other countries. Whatever happened subsequently, he was admired as one of the top few cricket personalities in the world.

News of his involvement in match fixing came as terrible shock and I know that he was as disappointed with his behaviour as anybody. There is no doubt that he deserved severe punishment but, as his 'trial' infolded in the full glare of publicity, I couldn't help feeling that he was being made a scapegoat.

It seemed some people were happy to see Hansie hung out to dry, while I thought he needed to be punished, to serve his time and then be rehabilitated into the game. There is an argument that says people of his calibre deserve to be handled with care and sensitivity. The new South Africa became known worldwide as a land of truth and reconciliation, but that did not, apparently, extend to Hansie.

The plane accident that claimed his life came as a second terrible blow to those of us who admired and respected him so much. I don't mind admitting I wept when I heard the news.

Hansie made a mistake. He was human. We all make mistakes. I have always been very proud to say Hansie Cronjé was a friend of mine. That never changed, and it never will. In 1998, after I had given the South African team some advice on their way to a series victory over the West Indies, I was given a silver tray engraved with the words, 'Thanks, Bunter, from the boys'. This kind of thoughtful gesture was typical of Hansie. I have given away most of the memorabilia from my career, but that tray stays on my bedside table. It is much too special to part with.

Another major factor in Free State's success was Corrie van Zyl. I called him '*Vonkelend*', because of the way his eyes sparkled when he laughed. He worked tremendously hard at his fast bowling, and was correctly rewarded with his Test cap on South Africa's historic tour to the Caribbean in 1992.

I reflected on that season with tremendous pleasure. As a coach, I don't think there is anything better than to work with players who are unconditionally eager to listen and learn. They started the campaign as no-hopers, and they finished as one of the most formidable teams in the country. In every sense, they were a genuine unit. Sure, we had our superstars – like Hansie and Allan Donald – but no individual thought he was more important than the team. The entire squad worked hard together, and they won together.

The Free State side of 1991/92 was an absolute joy to coach and, with the benefit of hindsight, maybe I should have continued coaching in Bloemfontein for longer. Instead, thinking the job was just about done, I was tempted further north by what seemed an even greater challenge.

Transvaal were traditionally the powerhouse province of South African cricket. Their team of the 1980s was as strong as any international side. They were known as the Mean Machine, and included world-class players like Jimmy Cook, Henry Fotheringham, Alvin Kallicharran, Graeme Pollock, Kevin Mackenzie, Clive Rice, Ray Jennings, Alan Kourie and Sylvester Clarke. Well, those days were past and, in 1992, the team was struggling to produce the kind of cricket expected by the demanding fans in Johannesburg. Invited to take over as the Transvaal coach, I enthusiastically signed on the dotted line and relished the new challenge.

The president of Transvaal cricket was Ray White, an old friend and rival from school days, and, as a former player of the province, I felt amongst friends. An informal cocktail party was held to mark my arrival, followed by a delicious curry dinner, and I looked forward to the new challenge.

It didn't require more than a couple of training sessions to make me realise that, with the number of quality players in our squad, we only needed to play to our ability and we would be fine. I was enthused, and delighted to have as my assistant coach Anton Ferreira. 'Yogi', as everyone knew him, was a very interesting character, with a great love of boxing. His proudest possession seemed to be a photograph of him facing Muhammad Ali, but he also knew his cricket and, in my view, we made an ideal combination.

Our first assignment of the 1992/93 season was a brief tour to England. It was going to be the first trip abroad by a South African provincial team since the end of international isolation, and I was determined that we would be excellent ambassadors, happily reflecting the demise of apartheid. Our tour group included cricketers of all races and, reflecting on my experiences in the 1960s, that made me very happy.

The team manager was Goolam Rajah, who acquitted himself admirably, and it was no surprise to me that he later advanced to fill the same role with the South African team for many years, with great success. Everything seemed to run smoothly with Goolam, and we never worried about a thing.

Jimmy Cook captained a squad that included Darryl Cullinan, Jack Manack, Hussein Manack, Steven Jack, Graeme Yates, Chad Grainger, Roy Pienaar, Anthony Pollock, Clive Eksteen, Bruce McBride, Brad White, Stephan Jacobs, Trevor Webster, Victor Vermeulen, and Matthew Vandrau.

I believed Jimmy was the ideal leader for a generally young team and, using his vast experience not only in Transvaal but also from his successful period with Somerset, so he proved.

Daryll Cullinan was the diamond in the side (pun intended). I used to call him 'Daniel', (from the lion's den) and there were times when I marvelled at his wonderful batting. He had every stroke in the book, and his memorable, unbeaten 337 against Northerns was undoubtedly one of the highlights of the season.

Every team has its irrepressible character, and ours was Stephen Jack. He was a brave fast bowler, with the wonderful nickname 'Charger'. He literally charged at everything, never stopped trying and, on his day, could be a formidable quickie, which led to his deserved selection for South Africa.

Watching this group of young South African cricketers assemble excitedly at the airport before travelling on tour overseas brought back so many memories of my own playing days, when we had flown off to Australia, and also to England.

The only difference was that we had no money, while these guys flashed their credit cards around the duty-free shops and emerged with all sorts of electronic equipment and a variety of 'ghetto blaster' music players.

The tour proved successful, and everybody enjoyed the privilege of playing the concluding match against an MCC team at Lord's. Even the younger players seemed impressed by the home of cricket.

We returned home and set about the challenge of the domestic season. My instinct about the quality of the players proved correct and, together with Yogi, we managed to get the team into shape. We were winning matches both in the first class competition and the one-day stuff, and all seemed well.

Transvaal was my third coaching assignment in four years, and I was growing accustomed to the routine of seeing a succession of eager young cricketers come and go, with me doing my best to help each on his way. With very few exceptions, they all appeared so enthusiastic, brave and optimistic, but, very sadly, while I was at Transvaal, one of these carefree youngsters was unexpectedly knocked back.

I remember the incident all too well. My mother was not very well and I had been visiting her in hospital, so I arrived at the Wanderers a few minutes later than usual, and met our team doctor, Len Weinstein.

"There's bad news, Eddie," he said, grimly. "Victor Vermeulen broke his neck at a party last night, and it seems as though he is paralysed."

"Where is he now?"

"He's at the Johannesburg General."

That was the hospital I had just left. I returned to the hospital later that afternoon and my mother passed away. It was a terrible day and I remember feeling in a complete daze, trying to come to terms with my own bereavement and the news of Victor's accident.

It transpired Victor has been performing his usual party piece of somersaulting into a swimming pool, but, somehow, his head had caught the edge of the pool. Typically, this exceptional young man came to terms with his condition and bounced back with real courage. He has now become an inspiring motivational speaker.

Well, the rest of us had to get back to the cricket, and we maintained our form. By the end of the season, we had put silverware in the Transvaal cupboard, and we maintained our progress in the following campaign.

It was, then, bitterly disappointing to learn that a Transvaal selector had seen fit to go behind my back and conduct a poll among the players to discover whether they wanted me to carry on as coach. By all accounts, he was surprised by the result: an overwhelming 'yes'.

The matter was allowed to drift. I returned to the Cape to spend the off-season on the farm, without really knowing what was going on. Would I return to Transvaal for another season or not? I didn't know. Dribs and drabs of information trickled through, but everything was handled very badly.

A Board meeting was held, where the members were led to believe I had formally resigned as coach. That was not the case but, for whatever reason, people were working against me. Petty politics is part of every large organisation, and I sensed I was caught in the crossfire of a boardroom struggle.

At any rate, I didn't go back for another season and, since I had not resigned, I suppose I must have been sacked, but nobody ever told me that was the case. It was ridiculous.

I remained on the farm, and started to believe the sour taste left by my treatment by Transvaal might signal the end of my involvement in cricket. In fact, after just a few months, I was lured back to the game by an offer to become Director of the Superjuice Academy for young cricketers in Paarl; and I am pleased I allowed myself to be tempted because this turned out to be one of the most rewarding periods of my life.

The concept was to create a joint Western Province/Boland cricket academy at the beautiful new stadium created for Boland cricket. It became a reality when Schalk Burger, a director of Megapro sports marketing, convinced Anton Rupert to provide sponsorship. The Superjuice Academy was born.

An old building adjacent to the new ground was completely refurbished, kitted out with indoor nets and full run-ups, and a series of different surfaces, which meant Academy players would be exposed to the same variation of spin and bounce that they would encounter on the field.

Both WP and Boland initially nominated 16 players to enrol at the Academy. There was much debate about racial quotas and affirmative action for black and coloured players at the time, but we went ahead and selected on merit and potential, and finished up with a nicely balanced mix of players.

There was a lesson. South Africans somehow have a great capacity for finding problems where none exist. So long as everyone's motives are honest and sincere – and I accept that is not always the case – a more relaxed approach to racial issues often produces a satisfactory outcome for everyone.

Our goal was straightforward: to produce cricketers for the national side. Some people said I was being too ambitious but there was no point in aiming low and, as Director, I started to develop programmes for our talented young men. We obviously focussed on batting, bowling, fielding and fitness, but we also included courses in topics such as captaincy, nurturing team spirit, dealing with the media and handling stress.

Some of my innovations were not successful. I had always been a keen student of the game, and thought the youngsters ought to be interested in hearing about the history of South African cricket. We assembled in the video room and, while showing archive film of past matches, I was happily discussing the merits of Neil Adcock, Graeme Pollock, Barry Richards and others when I developed an uneasy sense of being alone.

I turned up the lights to discover the students were all fast asleep. They were clearly much more interested in the future than the past, which, I suppose, is true of every generation.

Puma provided generous quantities of excellent kit and we made outstanding progress, to a point where the two provincial academy teams started playing regular matches. The Boland academy XI played at the Stellenbosch University field, and the WP academy side played their home matches at the lovely ground near the famous Constantia Uitsig wine estate, thanks to the generosity of my old friend and teammate, Dave McKay.

We encouraged the parents to feel involved, and I spent many happy hours walking around the boundary at Uitsig, chatting about their sons, and the academy. The mums and dads became part of the extended Superjuice Academy family and, even now, I smile as I remember the Marons, and their son Ryan, the Hofmeyrs (Simon), the Munniks (Renier), the Georges (Mulligan), the Bossengers (Wendell) and others.

It's wonderful how cricket brings people together. Some years later, I received a call from the police, asking me if I knew someone called Bossenger. It turned out there had been a serious car crash, and they were trying to contact the family, and my name had been found on a piece of paper in the car. We managed to help them and, thankfully, Pete Bossenger and his wife Nathalie both made a full recovery.

As time passed, I tried to expose the youngsters to more experienced competition, and we held our own against a few touring English county teams. I clearly recall Ryan Maron earning the respect of Eldine Baptiste, the West Indian all rounder, as he gleefully carted him all around the Uitsig ground.

Probably our most famous student was Paul Adams. When I first saw him bowl, the hairs on the back of my neck literally stood up like soldiers on parade. I believed we had found a spin bowler who could mean much to South African cricket for years to come, and, without any delay, I told the WP coaching staff about the naturally gifted young man who had suddenly emerged at the Academy.

The reply was depressing. "Eddie, we can't possibly use him," they said, in all seriousness. "If we picked a guy with an action like that, we'd be a laughing stock all over the country."

"Just give him a chance," I replied. "This guy is special."

His action was unusual. It was later described as being like a 'frog in a blender', but he had talent, and we continued to work with Paul at the Academy, until the sheer weight of his performances forced him into the WP provincial team and then, soon afterwards, into the South African side.

He was hailed as a phenomenon and his record in his first six months of international cricket was actually better than Shane Warne's record in the corresponding period, but somehow Paul never became the great Test spinner I believe he should have been. My personal view is that he was mishandled by a succession of coaches, but others will doubtless have their own opinion. It is, however, a great pity that a genuinely wonderful prospect, through no fault of his own, was allowed to fall by the wayside, and become less than he might have been.

The Superjuice Academy produced other excellent players. Eugene Moleon was a fine bowler, and a real charmer who used to entertain us with his mock radio commentaries. Young Wendell Bossenger was a very gifted wicketkeeper, who might easily have played for South Africa. Roger Telemachus and Charl Willoughby did emerge through the Academy and advance to represent their country at the highest level.

There were others who caught my eye: James Henderson, Wiaan Smit, Monet Villet, Renier Munnik, Mulligan George, Andrew Wylie and Andre Volsteedt all advanced to play provincial cricket.

Very sadly, my period with the Academy was curtailed by my personal circumstances. After separating from Julianne and leaving Bodega, I moved to the Windfall farm in Robertson, and it was just too far to travel between my new home and Paarl every day to fulfil my responsibilities with the youngsters.

I could hardly bring myself to tell the players that I was leaving. They had become my guys and somebody even called them 'Bunter's Babes'. We had worked so hard together. I hope the Academy continues to thrive and provide an important platform for emerging players in the two provinces.

My life seemed to be moving in ever-decreasing circles and, once again, I found myself returning to the farm and immersing myself in the business of farming. That was probably that with cricket, I thought … again; until, out of the blue, as usual, when I least expected it, the telephone at home started to ring.

It was my old mate, Mike Doherty, from Griqualand West. I hadn't spoken to him in years, so it was a nice surprise to hear from him again.

"Eddie, please man," he said. "Please come and coach Griquas. We're desperate."

My first reaction was that, this time, I would have to decline. Cally and I had just bought the farm near Robertson, and we had so much to do. Griquas were an historically small province trying to make it in the big time, and I just didn't feel I could spare enough time to do the job properly. I told Mike I was not in a position to help. He asked me to think about his proposal for a few days, and said he would call me back.

The challenge started to itch.

"What are you going to do?" Cally asked, one morning.

"I'm going to say no," I replied, firmly.

"Are you really?"

"Yes," I repeated. "I mean… no, I'm not going to do it."

She paused for a moment, and smiled.

After a while, she said: "You actually want to do it, don't you?"

My honest answer, deep down, was 'Yes'. The question was how, when we had so much to do to get things moving on Windfall. We decided to find a manager, and accept the job with Griquas, on the condition that we liked what was found when we flew up to Kimberley to have a look around.

There was a familiar face waiting to meet us at the airport: Fred Swarbrook, who had been my teammate at Derbyshire. He had been coaching the side, and I wasn't sure how he would feel about my arrival. I need not have worried, because he was evidently happy to hand me the reins. We spent the drive to our hotel laughing about the old days at Derbyshire and discussing the exciting potential at Griquas.

The meeting with Mike and Brian Kitson, the CEO, went well. The offer seemed fine, and they arranged for us to live in a house close to the De Beers ground. It was agreed I would start on 1 September, 1996.

We had some spare time that evening, and I decided to show Cally around the town. Kimberley had always seemed to me to have an air of the Wild West about it. That mood originated in the frenetic days of the diamond rush but, as we were to discover, the spirit was alive and well in the local cricket union. Our next task was to find a suitable farm manager and, after one false start, we eventually thought we had found a trustworthy person to look after Windfall while we were in Kimberley. I packed up the car, and headed north.

Well, we certainly got to know that road from Robertson to Kimberley well over the months that followed, and I must say I always enjoyed the drive because it followed a route right through the heart of this vast, untamed country that has always meant so much to me. Without wanting to sound too sentimental, even though I am a sentimental old sod, that drive seemed to revive my soul.

Straight up the N1 highway, through the Hex river valley, so beautiful in the autumn when the vines turned so many different shades of red... then through Touws River, which used to be the busy hub of the railway network but now seems to be resting peacefully... and then on through Laingsburg, the place where a flash flood rampaged through the town, killing some people in an old age home. I always seemed to notice the marker at the side of the road, which shows how high the water rose. It must have been terrifying.

Past the sleepy little *dorp* of Leeu Gamka, where Cally once got a speeding fine of R20, and on to the town of Beaufort West, the sheep capital of the Klein Karoo... then it was not long till the imposing koppies known as the Three Sisters, and the left turn towards Kimberley. We would pick up speed on the straight road carrying us past the towns of Victoria West, Britstown, Strydenburg and Hopetown, all in a blur, and then, at last, we would arrive in Kimberley, the Diamond city, which would, for this period, be our second home.

I set about the task at hand: developing the Griquas team. It was heartening to see two familiar faces at my first squad meeting. I first met Mickey Arthur at Free State, and knew him to be a thoroughly likeable young man and a fine batsman. He had moved to Griquas and been installed as captain. Wendell Bossenger was also there, and I was delighted to see the gifted wicketkeeper whom I knew from the Superjuice Academy.

Otherwise, the squad included Martin Gidley, a Brit who had settled in Kimberley, Willie Dry and a spinner called Pieter Barnard, who was also a *dominee* (priest). There was also Lungile Bosman from Galashewe, Finley Brooker, Craig Light, Andre Bothma, Cedric English, Adri Swanepoel, Deon Kreis and Garth Roe.

Our overseas player was Henderson Bryan, from Barbados, but I soon realised he was not fit. 'Hendy' was a lovely man, but we couldn't afford to keep him and he soon departed.

Well, maybe some of these guys were not going to set the world alight, but they were a decent bunch who wanted to work hard, learn and be successful. The mix was typical of what you might discover in any provincial cricket XI and, after all my years in the game, the types were becoming familiar: one was painfully shy, one was struggling in his father's shadow, one seemed to have a huge chip on his shoulder, one was a womaniser, one was as mad as a hatter and another one was just plain lazy. I liked every single one of them.

It was at this time that racial quotas were introduced in SA cricket, a doubtful policy designed to fast-track black and coloured players to the higher echelons of the game, but the regulations never posed any difficulties for us. Griquas benefited from a solid club structure, which had produced Lungile Bosman and Finley Brooker, both of whom would have made our team, with or without the quotas.

The team made excellent progress in that first season and I was very happy, give or take one or two furious selection meetings when Mike Doherty and I disagreed. 'Doc' had given most of his life to Griquas cricket, and he was rightly lionised by everyone at the union. I suppose that meant he was used to getting his way, but he should have known I was not the type to submit meekly to whatever he said.

We were mates of many years' standing, but maybe some conflict was inevitable. The standoff deteriorated during my second season in Kimberley and, unfortunately, it reached a point where I felt it was impossible for me to continue. I packed my bags and returned to the farm. That was that.

This proved to be the last time I coached in South Africa. I am proud of my record with Free State, with Transvaal, at the Superjuice Academy and at Griquas. Of course, there were ups and downs – and I'm sure some people will say I was a stubborn so-and-so – but I never gave less than my best and it is always rewarding when I meet a player, and he makes a point of telling me that I had helped him in his career.

As a coach, that's all I ever wanted to do.

Chapter Fifteen – Bangladesh Days

My life appeared to be moving in circles. I had imagined my departure from Griqualand West would signal the end of my involvement in cricket, but fate had another trick in store.

Out of the blue, the telephone rang on the farm. It was somebody from the United Cricket Board of South Africa, asking if I would accept a position as coach of the Bangladesh national team. My immediate response was that the UCB must really be desperate to get me out of the way.

Maybe that reaction was unfair, but it was 1999, and all sorts of rumours were circulating that I would never be given a chance to coach South Africa because, allegedly, the authorities reckoned I was too much trouble. Well, if an honest coach who speaks his mind is too much trouble, then they were right.

If not, they were wrong.

In fact, I never really contemplated coaching the Proteas, because the opportunity never arose. Some highly qualified people, including some players and journalists, were kind enough to say they reckoned I would have done a good job as national coach, but, as people often said, for some reason, I seemed to have become *persona non grata* at the UCB.

That was conjecture. The offer from Bangladesh was a fact.

"What do you know about Bangladesh?" I asked Cally.

"Not a lot, it used to be West Pakistan," she replied. "Why?"

"I've been asked to coach their national team."

She smiled. She had seen this film before. I had been adamant that, after Kimberley, there would be no more cricket. We would concentrate on the farm. Now, the siren was calling again.

"What do you think?" she asked, already knowing the answer.

"Well, it's international cricket," I said. "They are trying to get Test status. There's definitely potential there, but it would be a completely new culture, and…"

Cally added the rest: "And a new challenge."

"Exactly!"

We agreed that, at the very least, I would travel to the sub-continent and have a look around. There was some housekeeping to do first. Since Cally and I had both been married before, we had initially agreed that there was not much point getting married again. We were together, and that was all that mattered.

However, five years had passed, and after a long talk, we decided that, if we were going to spend time in a country like Bangladesh, it would be sensible to get properly and legally hitched. So we arranged a quiet ceremony at the Home Affairs office in Worcester. Mossie Henderson, the father of two of my Superjuice Academy players, accepted our invitation to be a witness, and he brought along a friend to complete the quota.

So it was done. We were married and, not long afterwards, I set off to see what this emerging cricket nation had to offer, genuinely excited by the prospect of this new adventure.

Bangladesh was never anything less. From the moment I arrived at bustling Dhaka airport, I was intoxicated by this remarkable country where 140 million people are squeezed into an area not much larger than Wales. Since gaining independence from Pakistan in 1971, the ordinary citizens appeared to have suffered an enormous amount of hardship, from bloody conflicts to various natural disasters.

As I soon discovered, to them, cricket represented something else. It offered hope.

I was met at the airport by one of the Bangladesh Cricket Board members, Ali Hasan Babu. He worked for the national airline and, having smoothed my path through customs, drove me to meet Saber Hossain Chowdhury, the President of the BCB and a member of parliament. He outlined his Board's ambitions to be granted full Test status by the International Cricket Council, and arranged a quick tour.

We visited BKSP, a beautifully appointed school for sporting excellence that reminded me of Millfield School, in England, and also the vast Bangabandu National Stadium, named after Sheik Mujib Rahman, who was respected as the father of the nation. His daughter, Sheik Hasina, was the Prime Minister.

The facilities were less than impressive, but the passion for the game was unmistakable. Almost everywhere we went, we saw groups of eager youngsters enjoying impromptu games of cricket.

"This place is cricket mad," I told Babu, incredulously.

"You're right," he replied. "So will you help us?"

The answer was yes and I accepted the position.

Incidently, I had cut myself quite badly on the foot before this initial trip to Bangladesh and, as my recce had progressed, the condition of the wound seriously deteriorated. It became so bad and painful that I actually needed to be pushed around in a wheelchair when I flew home. That was somewhat ironic, in view of what lay ahead of me.

Yet again, we had to find a manager for the farm. That did not prove an easy task but we were delighted to employ Pauli Viljoen and, after putting what seemed a reasonable structure in place, eventually, in July 1999, Cally and I arrived to start our new lives in Bangladesh.

A comfortable flat had been arranged for us, even though the air conditioning was temperamental from the moment we arrived until the day we left. Everybody we met was extremely kind and we gradually settled into our new lifestyle, getting used to the new sights and smells that surrounded us.

The traffic in Dhaka was something else, and amazing to behold: a crazy, raucous bustle of highly decorated cycle rickshaws, baby taxis with fixed canopies, slightly larger so-called tempos, battered cars that were difficult to identify because parts were missing, roaring 4 x 4s for the elite, fume-belching lorries and buses that appeared to be driven like tanks, completely oblivious of anyone and anything in their path; and in the middle of all this, now and then, a cart from the rural areas, being pulled either by a man or an ox.

With all these vehicles on the road, we used to wonder how the traffic ever moved. We soon discovered that, very often, it didn't. Then the gridlock produced a chorus of shouting and horns, with quarrelling drivers eager to jump out of their cars and exchange blows. The entertainment was non-stop.

It was Michael Holding, the West Indian fast bowler, who once noted:

"The traffic lights in Dhaka are merely decorative." He was right. Nobody pays a blind bit of attention to them.

My first meeting with the national squad took place at a training camp, which proved an ideal environment for me to identify our various strengths and weaknesses. It was impossible not be impressed by the real commitment of the group, as I worked hard to familiarise myself with each of the players.

The leaders were Naimur Rahman, generally known as DJ... captain, No.4 batsman, right-arm off-spinner; and Khaled Masud, called Pilot... vice-captain, wicket keeper, solid middle-order batsman.

There were some decent top order batsmen, like Javed Omar Belim, Shariar Hossain and Mehrab, but it was clear we would need some new stars to emerge... like Ehasanul Hoque who had spent time at the Plascon Academy, in South Africa, and showed promise, or a talented, fluent top order batsman named Habibul Bashar, and known to everyone as Sumon, or a young lad called Ashraful, who looked a fantastic prospect.

There was so much talent and potential. The challenge for me, as coach, was to sort the Test quality wheat from so much eager, but not quite good enough chaff. It was not going to be easy. My task was not to find five or six batsmen from, say, 10. I was looking for five or six from a hundred possibles.

Hoque, known as Moni, proved an accurate left-arm spin bowler, who would be able to do a decent job for us but, in contrast to the wealth of batsmen, I was struggling to find any all-rounders or fast bowlers, who would be able to lead our attack. A nationwide search was required.

I had made one request to the Bangladesh authorities, specifically that I would be able to bring a top fitness coach from South Africa to improve the squad's physical conditioning. I had come across Gavin Benjafield at the SA Sports Science Institute in Cape Town, and he accepted the job. Gavin developed a programme to develop the players' strength, and proved a source of fantastic support in many ways.

The weeks began to roll by, and I was enjoying the challenge, but some familiar problems did arise. I began to detect some degree of patronage in the selection process whereby, for some or other reason, usually a family tie, particular players seemed protected and preserved in the national team. Needless to say, favouritism was not going to wash with me, and I insisted the team be chosen on merit alone.

I found the Board supportive, with the exception of one member who made no secret of his conviction that I simply did not belong in his country. We had an open and frank exchange of views.

Selection meetings also presented their own frustrations, largely because the selection committee members were voluntary, unpaid and laden with other responsibilities.

The Chairman of Selectors actually attended no more than a handful of matches. He was eager, but just didn't have the time. As a result, our deliberations in selecting the national team sometimes assumed farcical proportions.

"We must play X," one of the selectors would declare. "He's a very good player."

I would ask: "But do you really think he is as good as Y?"

The same selector would reply: "Oh no, you're right… Y is much better."

"OK," I would say, "so, who are you going to drop?"

Blank faces all round. I was supposed to be only attending as an advisor, but these selection meetings in Bangladesh proved to be the longest and most exhausting of my entire career, and they always seemed to start an hour late. Eventually, somehow, we ended up with a team that looked respectable.

In a new environment, I was fortunate to find two individuals who always seemed willing to do that little bit extra and make my life easier: Dipu Roy Chowdhury was a former national team fast bowler, and nothing was too much trouble for this character with flashing eyes and a big black beard, who reminded me of Desperate Dan from the comics; and an ever-smiling man whom everyone called 'Joy' did a wonderful job in looking after and feeding the team at our training complex.

A twin strategy emerged specifically to identify and maximise available talent in the national squad, and to create structures and programmes to enhance the game at grass roots level. I regarded both tasks as critical to the future of the cricket in Bangladesh, and embraced them equally.

At elite level, first and foremost, the national team needed regular competition where raw, naturally talented players could get accustomed to the special pressures of the international game. There was no substitute for being out in the middle, and I proposed a ten-year programme of incoming and outgoing tours.

I wanted to expose these cricketers to different conditions all around the world, and give them the chance to develop and gain confidence. The process was going to take time. There were no short cuts, as I often had to tell Board members who expected a complete Test team to emerge overnight.

The task at grass roots was just as exciting. Our challenge was not to stimulate demand for cricket, but to meet the demand, as I was regularly reminded every single morning when, walking to my car in the garage under our flat, I would have to pick a path through youngsters batting and bowling.

We arranged for cricketing manuals to be translated into Bengali and distributed in rural areas, empowering more and more people to learn the basic techniques. I even picked up some useful phrases, myself, and was soon to be found, shouting Shabbash (well done) at anyone who did something right.

It was fun. We were working hard, setting a healthy pace. Whenever the national squad was not gathered, or there were no club games to watch, we organised visits to other parts of the country, developing programmes, encouraging coaches, and identifying facilities that needed attention.

During these trips I started to notice a substantial number of unused gyms in various cities and towns, and suggested these could be converted into indoor nets during the rainy season. When the monsoon strikes, most of the land surface was flooded and playing cricket became impossible. My concept met with an enthusiastic response, and we were starting to kit out some of the first of these gyms.

There was no doubt we were making progress, but the overriding aim was to secure full Test status, and it became clear that Bangladesh would have to satisfy the requirements of the ICC in two areas: the national team would have to prove that they would be able to hold their own at the highest level of the game, and the country would need to develop the infrastructure to support fully-fledged Test cricket.

We needed to prove ourselves, on the field and off the field, and an MCC tour at the end of 1999 provided an opportunity to measure our progress in developing a decent national team.

This MCC touring squad was not 'the' England team, but a respectable group from the Marylebone Cricket Club under the management of Colonel John Stephenson, a real stalwart of the game and a wonderful character whom I had met several times. The series of matches offered a real opportunity.

Amazingly, as our visitors arrived, certain members of our Board provoked a pay dispute with the players and, after initially trying to keep out of the fight, I couldn't resist getting involved.

"Listen," I told the Board. "Without the players, you don't have a team. And without a team, you won't get Test status. It's as simple as that. Let's sort this out and get on with the cricket."

Sanity prevailed and, as I had expected, the players rose to the occasion. The quality of their performance was not reflected in the results, and the Englishmen came out on top, but we had proved our potential. As I later learned, the MCC side took a positive message back to Lord's.

Our case was looking strong off the field as well. The country could offer three Test venues: in Dhaka, in the major port of Chittagong, and in Rajshahi, the hub of the silk industry; and there were ample practice facilities to meet the demands of international touring teams. We were ticking all the boxes and, as I travelled around the country, I started to sense a real mood of excitement and expectation among the people.

"Do you think we'll get Test status," everybody asked.

"I hope so," I replied, smiling, wanting to look confident.

"Are we ready?"

"Yes, of course, we are."

The crunch came with the visit of an official ICC Inspection team, which would have a look around and then make a recommendation to the full Council, one way or the other. The same trio of cricket people had visited the previous year and provided a detailed list of issues that needed to be addressed. Some of these had been done, others were in progress, and a few were still on the drawing board.

Perhaps understandably, the Board were eager to host the ICC officials themselves and, as the tour started, I kept a discreet distance from the discussions. That was right and proper.

As it happened, I had known two members of the ICC group for many years: Andy Pycroft was an energetic Zimbabwean who often used to attend the nets at Western Province; and I had played against Graham Dowling, the New Zealander. The third was an intelligent man called Nasim ul Ghani, from Pakistan, and I had had dealings with him in his capacity as the ICC's development officer in our region.

A day or two passed. Then, I received a telephone call from one of the inspectors.

"Eddie, we're not being shown the things we want to see," he said. "If you want Test status, we had better start being shown what matters, and it needs to happen quickly."

I immediately contacted the President of the Board, and explained the situation. He asked me to revise the itinerary, take charge of hosting the visit and get things back on track. It was hectic and frenetic, but we were all cricketing people, and we started to address the issues, one by one.

Some concern was expressed about the quality, rather than the size, of the Test venues, and I responded by explaining that the finishing touches to upgrade the facilities required more investment, and that that would come from the sponsorship deals that would certainly follow the granting of Test status. We were in a chicken-and-egg situation, and I repeatedly asked the ICC group to concentrate on the potential.

I desperately wanted to remind Graham that the pitches we had played on 30 years before in New Zealand certainly had not matched up to my idea of Test grounds and nobody had queried the Kiwis' entry into the Test arena, but decided that such a chirp might not be appropriate at that particular moment.

Our message seemed to be getting through and, as we bade farewell at the airport, I was starting to believe that, after all the challenges of getting the various elements of Bangladesh cricket to work together and pull in the same direction, our goal of gaining full Test status was finally within sight.

The ICC would consider all the evidence and, we were informed, make their final decision in June 2000.

By then, my life had been changed forever.

Chapter Sixteen – Tough Days

Everything changed on 29 April, 2000.

That afternoon, I went shopping with Cally in Dhaka. I wasn't feeling myself and in fact at one stage I had to sit down just to take a breather. Maybe I had caught a bug. It didn't seem serious.

We went home to our flat, and both settled in the living room. Cally was reading; I was sipping a beer. As I drank, one gulp seemed to slip down the wrong way, so I stood and walked through to the kitchen to get a paper towel. I remember absolutely nothing about the four hours that followed.

Cally told me later that, after a minute or so, she wondered where I was and called out to me. There was no reply, so she called again and, this time, heard a curious noise. She leaped to her feet, and discovered I had fallen down beside the fridge. She tried to help me up, but I was too heavy.

"I just need a little help," I told her.

It was impossible to move me. I was stuck. Cally could see the left side of my body was paralysed, and she was beginning to fear I had suffered some kind of stroke. She phoned Gavin Benjafield, the South African fitness trainer who had come with us to Bangladesh, and asked him to come straight over. He arrived and together they managed to get me down to the car, and drove me to our doctor.

Cally then dashed back to the flat and phoned Saber Chowdhury, President of the Bangladesh Cricket Board, to tell him what had happened. He responded immediately and must have pulled some strings to get me admitted to Dhaka's Military Hospital, a place usually reserved for government officials.

Once I had been admitted, I was given a thorough medical examination, taken for a CAT scan and then put in the private room that I was to occupy for the next ten days. Everything had happened so quickly. One minute, I was walking around. The next minute I was on my back, wondering if I would die.

It was a frightening experience, of course, but, as I became accustomed to my surroundings, my instinctive reaction was to roll up my sleeves and say: 'Right, what's the plan to put this right'. That was the way I had dealt with most obstacles in my life, but this was different. There was no quick fix.

The doctors wore full army uniform, and only the stethoscopes around their necks suggested they were anything other than regular officers, but they were tremendously professional and kind. In fact, everybody in the hospital was friendly and helpful, and the entire place was spotless.

Two day later, an MRI scan revealed exactly what had happened. I had suffered a mega-stroke of the right front temporal lobe of my brain. The pattern of such strokes is that it is the opposite side of the body that suffers the effects, and this explained why my left flank, arm and leg were all paralysed. My capacity to speak had hardly been affected, so, for that mercy at least, Cally and I were both grateful.

Our friends in Dhaka rallied in support. Barbara Epworth, Clare Lemon, Kate Dixon, Carloyn Meyrick and Joy Lewer formed a meal rota, and produced a regular supply of lasagne, soups, biscuits and other meals, all of which made a welcome change from the daily diet of tasty, but similar, hospital curries.

Barbara even managed to slip past the tight hospital security and sit with me now and then, giving Cally a deserved break. Gavin was also a fantastic source of support, coming to visit and keeping me abreast of the latest cricket developments. "Don't worry," I told him, "I'll be back."

Looking back, it was a terrible time – for the first few days, it seems nobody was quite sure whether I would live or die – but we just got on with what had to be done. We came through the crisis. There was no option. Cally and I had faced tough times before, on the farm and in cricket, and we simply battled on together.

It didn't take long for us to agree it would be easier for me to undergo my rehabilitation in South Africa and, after consulting with the doctors in Dhaka, it was arranged that, rather than fly straight home, we would break the tiring long-haul journey with a stopover at a hospital in Singapore.

Well, that turned out to be some place. The Mount Elizabeth hospital, just a stone's throw from the shopping centres of Orchard Road, was equipped with a special stroke unit and the latest equipment. Everything looked very swish, and I was introduced to my new medic, Dr Chang.

Work began the following day, when I was hurled into the deep end of my rehabilitation. We were told there would be three types of physiotherapy: ordinary, occupational and speech; and I had one session of each brand in the morning, and another session of each in the afternoon: six in the day.

One of the Singaporean physiotherapists was called Fiona, and she took no nonsense. I quite enjoyed their business-like approach, and looked forward to the challenge.

"Hip to rip, Eddie," she said, giving me instructions of what to do.

"Sorry?"

"Come on, come on. Hip to rip!"

"What?"

I had no idea what she meant, and it required the assistance of one Fiona's colleagues for me to understand she was saying: 'Hip to rib'. That was fine. It was sore, but I just about managed.

Cally was staying at an hotel up the road and, one evening, she brought me a plate of oysters covered in ice. That was a real treat, and it proved that, so long as we were together and we stayed positive, even in these rough periods, we could still enjoy the little pleasures that make life worthwhile. Staying positive: that was the key, and we both gained strength from watching other victims face the same challenges.

Every morning, Cally would arrive and lead me through some of my speech exercises, making me repeat the vowels in order and out loud, with exaggerated pronunciation.

"Aaaaa, Eeeee, Iiiii, Ooooo, Uuuuu," I said.

"Again," she barked, grinning.

"Aaaaa, Eeeee, Iiiii, Ooooo, Uuuuu," I repeated.

All of a sudden, we heard a voice from behind the curtain repeat the five vowels in exactly the same way. It turned out to be the Chinese gentleman in the next bed. His wife's face peeked around the curtain, and she was grinning broadly. "Thank you," she beamed. "That's the first time he has spoken since his stroke."

We both smiled as well.

Trying to get myself into a comfortable position was still a regular and incredibly frustrating chore, because my shoulder was still terribly bruised and sore, but Cally found three small pillows in a local shop, and these made a real difference. I didn't let them out of my sight, and we became firm friends.

After ten days in Singapore, Dr Chang reckoned I was stable enough to withstand the flight back home to South Africa, and we bade farewell to him, Fiona and other staff at the Mount Elizabeth. Too many us take medical staff for granted, and only appreciate what they do when we are in desperate need. I had arrived at their front door in a pretty bad way, but I left with a renewed determination that, at the very least, I would walk again.

The flight to South Africa passed without any incident, and I was booked into a room at the Constantiaberg Medicentre in Cape Town, thanks to the efforts of Kelly Seymour, my Springbok teammate from 1970. It was neither the first nor the last time that one of my old mates came up trumps.

I enjoyed being back among familiar surroundings, but the rehabilitation programme started to feel like a rollercoaster ride. One day we were up, the next day we were down.

One day a doctor took Cally to one side and told her I would not walk again. The next day, I moved my toes and he said that wouldn't make any difference. A couple of days later, I managed to raise my foot off the bed. He promptly declared that made all the difference and I could probably walk again.

Professor Peter Jacobs, my haematologist, was a gem. He arrived one day and told me, with a straight face, that there had been a coup in Bangladesh, and the new President had banned cricket. I was stunned, and it took me a couple of minutes to realise he was joking. Laughter is the best medicine.

Hylton Ackerman did his bit as well. By a strange quirk of fate, while I was lying in my hospital bed in Cape Town, Dutchman was similarly incarcerated in a Johannesburg hospital. Our wives and doctors thanked their lucky stars we were not in the same ward, but we did speak on the phone.

"Hey," I told him. "I'm learning to walk again."

"What do you mean?"

"I'm in rehab. I'm learning to walk again."

He retorted: "You've never walked in your life. You must be ill."

Still, there were ups and downs. One day, I was making excellent progress with Sally, one of my physiotherapists. The next day, I fell off the loo while trying to reach the bell, toppled off the throne and opened a gash on my forehead, which just kept bleeding. One day, I thought I had some feeling back in my left side. The next day, my left arm felt completely useless again.

One day, at Molly Wilson's physiotherapy practice, I felt euphoric as, at last, with the help of a special harness, and Jenny, Laurie and Anne, the physios, I managed to stand on my own feet,. The next day, I had to have some blood tests at a new hospital, and was subjected to an inquisition by an insensitive doctor.

Always ups and downs but, as the days passed, I sensed the ups were more frequent than the downs, and nothing raised my spirits as much as the visits by friends. Pete Eedes, my old friend from Boys High, came to see me with his wife Jennie; so did Peter and Gary Kirsten, and many others.

We were making real progress. When the doctors said Cally could take me out for the day, we went for lunch with Mignon and Cas van Wyk and their sons in Paarl. A week after that, it was decided I could leave hospital and we celebrated the red letter day by taking Kelly and Sarah Seymour to dinner at Peddlers, in Constantia. The Seymours had allowed Cally to be their lodger for almost a month, so she could stay near the hospital. They had proved themselves to be the ultimate friends in need.

A million miles away, or so it seemed, the ICC met in London, discussed the report from the Inspection visit and duly voted to award full Test status to Bangladesh. I was thrilled for everybody in Dhaka, especially for all the players who had worked so hard. My overwhelming target was to complete my rehabilitation, get back to Dhaka as soon as possible, and then to complete the work we had started before my stroke.

We returned to our farm, Windfall, and Cally said: "OK, let's make a deal."

"What deal?"

"We'll go back to Bangladesh as soon as you can walk from your seat on the plane to the loo."

"Deal," I agreed.

More physiotherapy followed, but I now I had a clear goal, and this was very much on my mind when I was taken to see yet another physiotherapist, Rita Viviers, in Robertson.

"So when can I start walking," I blurted out.

Rita's reply was brilliant: "Well, let's try now."

She helped me from my wheelchair to the side of the bed, and then pulled me forward until I was standing on my own, wobbling a little but standing nonetheless. Clutching a quad stick in my good right hand and with Rita supporting my left side, I took one step... then another... then another.

I can't explain how much those small steps meant for me. In that moment, after all the pain and discomfort, all the concern and worrying, all the uncertainty, I knew for sure that I would walk again. I was not going to be confined to a wheelchair for the remainder of my life after all.

We worked relentlessly for the eight weeks that followed. Rita goaded me through an hour's exercise every Monday, Wednesday and Friday. Cally pushed me on Tuesdays, Thursdays and Saturdays and this pair of tough taskmistresses generously agreed that I would be allowed to rest on Sundays.

Still more ups and downs. One day, I felt ready to drive to the airport and fly back to Bangladesh; next day my shoulder was so sore, I just wanted to get into bed and sleep.

At last, by mid-August, four months after the stroke, we reached a decision that we were ready to return to our lives in Bangladesh... but only after a short holiday *en route* to the sub-continent, first with Cally's daughter Fiona and her family in Jersey, and then with her son Alasdair and his family in England. I just about managed to negotiate the stairs in both houses, and the break did us both the world of good.

Simply arriving back in Bangladesh felt like a major achievement for both of us, and I felt quite emotional when I spotted the smiling face of Ali Hasan Babu in the crowd at the airport. He took us out to the car, where our driver, Farouk, was also grinning. We arrived back at the flat and found our maid, Shehara, waiting. She was not smiling because there were torrents of tears pouring down her cheeks.

"So good to see you," she said, repeatedly stroking my arm.

We were back, and I was ready to resume where I had been so rudely interrupted. I met with the President of the Board, Saber Chowdhury, and congratulated him on securing Test status. He told me again and again how delighted he was to see me back, and how much he wanted me to help the national team.

I took him at his word. It was an exciting time, counting the days down to Bangladesh's first ever five-day Test match, against India in Dhaka. That was going to be some occasion.

Looking back, maybe I was naïve to think it would be possible for us to return and find everything as we had left it four months before. Life is not like that. Situations develop, and people change.

Time had not stood still and it soon became clear that, spotting a gap caused by my absence, several individuals had mounted their campaigns to ingratiate themselves with the hierarchy and move into my areas of responsibility.

There was, I sensed, a different mood. Assistant coaches and development officers who had previously been eager for guidance were now telling me how much they had achieved, and how well it was going. They seemed to have stopped listening. Was this because they watched me struggling in and out of my wheelchair, and assumed I would battle to coach cricket as well? Be patient, I told myself.

Give them time to adapt to the new situation and, in time, they would grow to understand that, even if I did not bustle around as before, my cricket brain was just the same as ever.

It was a difficult time, I won't deny it, but there was no time to sit and worry because the Bangladesh team were about to set off on tour to play a one-day tournament in Kenya and then some matches in South Africa, as part of their preparations for the big time. After some discussion, it was agreed that I would join the touring group not as the coach, but as an observer. Cally would come along, as my minder.

The tour, sad to say, was a disaster from start to finish. Arrangements were poor, punctuality flew out the window, the coaching structure was confused and lacked authority; and, as a result, the poor players performed far below their potential, and were repeatedly thrashed on the field.

I tried to help put things right, at one stage running around like a scalded cat, figuratively but not literally, to secure the proper visas for South Africa, because they had not been arranged, but my view has always been that the coach should be left to get on with the job of coaching the side, and I was determined not to interfere.

Of course it was frustrating. There were many times when I would have loved to have jumped out of that wheelchair, and bustled around, getting everything shipshape, but that was not possible.

On a personal level, Cally and I enjoyed the South African leg of the tour, because we were able to catch up with old friends in Kimberley, then in Bloemfontein, Pietermaritzburg and Durban; and, everywhere we went, the people were extremely generous and pleased to see me back in cricket.

In fact, the coach of the SA Invitation XI we played at Kingsmead, in Durban, turned out to be none other than Hylton Ackerman, and Dutchman and I spent some time together, when he pushed me in my wheelchair to the Marine Parade, and we chatted for a while. It all seemed a long way from the days when I ran back up that hill in Stellenbosch because he had got lost during a training run.

The team returned to Bangladesh in a sorry state, and inevitably the recriminations started. Everybody was blaming everyone else, and I started to feel peripheral within the structure. I still retained excellent relations with many of the players, and almost all of these eager cricketers sought me out for a private word of guidance here or there, but it was a handful of officials who seemed to have a problem with me.

Important meetings were held, and I only heard about them afterwards. At one point, a journalist called the flat and asked me to explain my precise role. I couldn't give him an answer.

Time moved on and I began to form the view that, so far as the Bangladesh Cricket Board were concerned, I had served my purpose. They had needed an established cricket person to help them secure their Test status but, once that had been achieved, they felt they didn't need me anymore.

Yet I was still there and still being paid. I explained how, even with restricted mobility, I could help motivate the team, and complete the grass roots projects we had started, but it was no good.

At one low point I remember telling Cally: "Let's face it. They don't want Barlow here and, you know what, they certainly don't want Barlow in a wheelchair. That's the way it is."

Even amid all this uncertainty and frustration, I could not avoid feeling genuinely excited about the prospect of the inaugural Test against India.

I suppose once cricket gets into your blood, it stays there. There were butterflies in my stomach. It was just like the old days. These were my boys, players whom I had grown to appreciate, and, as I arrived at the ground, I desperately hoped they would do themselves justice.

For three and a half days, they did precisely that. When DJ won the toss and decided to bat, Bangladesh made exactly 400 in their first innings of Test cricket, with Aminul Islam and Bulbul making centuries. India replied with a similar first innings score and, just when the crowd was starting to believe an unimagined victory was possible, the local heroes collapsed in their second innings, and subsided to defeat.

"What happened, Eddie?"

"Where do we go from here, Mr Barlow?"

As we left the ground, all sorts of people kept approaching me and asking for an explanation. I told them to be patient and that, just like Rome, Test-playing countries were not built in a day.

Still, the second innings collapse disappointed me. It almost seemed as if someone had told the batsmen to be cautious, and keep half an eye on simply trying to survive and hold out for a draw. That was fatal. If there was one thing I learned in half a century of playing cricket, it was that you must always be positive.

In any event, my ongoing discussions with the BCB reached a stage where they informed me I could work as Director of Development and take a salary cut, or resign. Cally and I accepted the latter option, so we packed up and, after some very emotional goodbyes, travelled home to South Africa.

We had loved our period in Bangladesh and, despite the shenanigans with the Board when we returned after my stroke, we really cherished the friends we made. Four years later, in 2004, we met up with the players before they played a Test against England at Lord's, and it was fantastic to see them all again.

At this point, I suppose it would nice to reflect that we returned to our farm in Robertson, that I found some coaching work here and there to keep me busy, that we found a reliable farm manager who helped us produce our wine, and that Cally and I were able to enjoy a quiet retirement.

Sadly, that didn't happen, and we were made to endure further trials.

There seemed to be no coaching opportunity for me in South African cricket, which was demoralising. One provincial president sounded encouraging at one stage, and said my ability should never be wasted, and that there was a job for me, that he would call me back... but he never did.

Our misfortune with farm managers continued, and, somehow, it even seemed impossible for us to sell the substantial volume of high quality wine that was still stored on the farm.

Then we became embroiled in a dispute with our insurance company, who refused to pay my medical bills because, according to them, they were unaware that I suffered from high blood pressure. My brother Norman came to our assistance, and negotiated for the company to meet at least some of the costs, but our financial situation was becoming extremely serious. I wondered when we would get a break.

Hylton Ackerman came up with the idea of staging a Benefit Evening for me, where the great and the good of South African cricket and rugby, past and present, would gather and generate funds.

I was hesitant, at first, because I have never wanted to be someone who puts out their hand, but, in fact, it turned out to be one of the most wonderful evenings of my life.

When everyone had arrived and taken their seats, Dutchman pushed me into the room in my wheelchair to the sound of applause. Then I managed to get to my feet and walk the last few steps to my seat, on my own. It was a battle, and I may only have been off a short run but, man, I made it.

Everywhere I looked, there was an old friend, either from school or university, from rugby or cricket, from farming or politics. Cally and I had been through some tough times, but it was humbling and heartening to feel so much warmth from so many people, who really cared about us. Almost the entire South African team from the 1970 series against Australia were sitting at our table, and, as somebody said to me the next day, it was fantastic to see so many good people gathered together in one room.

Ironically, amid all the overwhelming kindness, the reality was that Cally and I had reached rock bottom. We sat there, the centre of attention, wondering what would become of us.

I remember, the following morning, we sat together and had what I always used to call a 'team talk', where we made an honest assessment of our situation, and developed a game plan. The hard facts were these... I had no job in South Africa, and seemed unlikely to find one; we had not been able to find a market-related buyer for the farm, and would probably have to accept a low price; debts were mounting.

"Maybe we should go and live in the UK," Cally said. She had spoken to her brother David, who suggested we do exactly that and look after her mother who was elderly. At least we would have a roof over our heads and perhaps I might get some work there. It was a lifeline.

"OK," I said. "If we get rid of the farm at an auction, the money raised at the benefit should cover our debts. We could leave without owing anything to anyone, and make a fresh start."

It was a major step but, thinking it over, it seemed to me, this was the only option; and, over the months that followed, this was exactly the plan that we put into action. 'Windfall' was sold at auction, and I started to put out some feelers to find a coaching job in North Wales. I telephoned Tony Lewis, who put me in contact with a man called John Huband. It was John's responsibility to run the development network in North Wales, so I called him and outlined my position, and he responded by saying he was sure they would find something for me.

"Just give us a call when you get here," he finished.

At last we seemed to be getting somewhere and, having secured my entry visa by virtue of the fact that my grandparents had both been British citizens, we booked our flights.

I have never much enjoyed leaving South Africa – it's my country, and I love the place – but this particular departure was the hardest of all, partially because it seemed so final but also because we had both had to come to terms with the heart-wrenching fact that we were unable to take our pets with us.

Our two dogs, Sweep and Sooty, and the cats, ffrench and Portsmiff, one with a double 'f' at the beginning, the other with a double 'f' at the end, had been part of our family for nearly five years, and it is hard to describe our feelings when Cally took them to be put to sleep. I chickened out of this horrible task. On the day we left Windfall for the last time, Cally and I stood by their graves, which the staff had decorated with flowers, and wept.

We left South Africa in the middle of summer, and pitched up in North Wales in the middle of winter, but we were soon warmed by the welcome in the town of Ruthin. I arranged to meet John Huband, who proved as good as his word. Within a fortnight I was employed as a part-time coach for the North Wales Cricket Development Board. At last I was working and we could start living again.

Initially, I needed to have Cally around, to push me in the wheelchair to the bowler, when I wanted to talk to him, then back to the batsman, when I needed to make a point to him.

This was not ideal, not least for Cally, but the Professional Cricketers Association came to our aid. They had heard about my predicament, and through Peter Walker and David Graveney, the English PCA provided me with an electric scooter, which effectively gave me back my legs. All of a sudden I was mobile again and I had that bit of independence that I had craved ever since the stroke.

Organisations like the PCA may not get too much publicity or credit, but they made a massive difference to my life when it seemed that nobody else really cared. I will forever be grateful, especially to David and Peter who took a special interest in me, and ensured that the electric scooter arrived.

I coached the Ruthin team initially but the following season there was an invitation to help the Marchwiel and Wrexham team, who were playing in the Premier League. I eagerly accepted, and was made to feel wonderfully welcome by John Bell, the club president, Peter Furber, the Chairman, and Frank Gibson, with whom I spent many happy hours passing the time and talking about cricket.

Cally and I settled happily in Wales, and adapted to the gentle rhythm of the place. After all the difficulties, it felt good to be secure and surrounded by friends. Now and then we embarked on trips to Derbyshire, where I saw old friends, or watched Test matches at Lord's, where we were always well looked after by Roger Knight, the MCC Secretary, and Tim Rice, when he was President of the Club.

We returned to South Africa to watch the ICC World Cup in 2003, courtesy of the Wanderer's Club, and my old friend Peter Cooke looked after us extremely well. It was good to see my daughter Susan again, when she flew up from Cape Town.

On a subsequent trip back to Cape Town, we met my son Craig, who was by then living in Malawi, and his new wife, Diana.

Otherwise, we remained in Wales, enjoying each day as it came and looking forward to the next time we saw Cally's three grandsons, Henry, Ruaridh and Hamish. They are three very special little men, and, now that they were just starting to get interested in cricket, I could not resist contacting Gray Nicholls and asking them to send me three junior bats, three junior boxes and three junior pairs of gloves.

We carted all this stuff over to Jersey, where we going to spend Christmas with Cally's daughter, Fiona, and her family. As soon as we arrived, I couldn't resist rummaging around in our luggage for the bats.

Cally asked: "Aren't you going to wait till Christmas Day?"

"Oh no," I replied. "I can't wait that long. I want to see how they shape up now."

It was freezing cold, but I sat on a chair in the garden, with a warm rug tucked over my lap, and spent an hour or so instructing the boys on the basics of batting and bowling.

Every minute was a pleasure for me, and the boys seemed to enjoy it as well. It started to snow. We kept playing.

That's me… a cricketer until the very end.

Appendix A

FAVOURITES

It is a traditional feature of many cricket books that the author is allowed to choose his favourite grounds and players. Well, I am eager to indulge myself in this respect.

My favourite ground has always been Newlands because it is so beautiful and I enjoyed so many happy days there, first as a player and latterly as a spectator. My least favourite ground is Kingsmead in Durban, for no other reason than that I never seemed to do particularly well there. My favourite foreign ground would have to be Adelaide, again because I scored freely there.

My favourite opponents were the Australians, because they seemed so professional and committed... at the end of every Test against them, we knew we had been in a tough fight.

Last, here are two teams to play the ultimate Test, an all-time South African XI against an all-time Rest of the World team:

My all-time South African Test team

1. Barry Richards
2. Jackie McGlew
3. Peter Kirsten
4. Graeme Pollock
5. Dennis Lindsay
6. Eddie Barlow
7. Denys Hobson
8. Hugh Tayfield
9. Mike Procter
10. Peter Heine
11. Neil Adcock

My all-time Rest of the World Test team (excluding South Africans)

1. Jack Hobbs
2. Len Hutton
3. Donald Bradman
4. Richie Benaud
5. Gary Sobers
6. Ian Botham
7. Bob Taylor
8. Shane Warne
9. Derek Underwood
10. Michael Holding
11. Wes Hall

Appendix B

Eddie Barlow's Career Record

All First-class Matches

M	Inns	NO	Runs	HS	Avg	100	50	Ct	St	Balls	Runs	Wkts	Avg	RPO	BB	5I	10M
283	493	28	18212	217	39.16	43	86	335	0	31930	13785	571	24.14	2.59	7-24	16	2

First-class matches for Provincial/County teams

Team	M	Inns	NO	Runs	HS	Avg	100	50	Ct	St	Balls	Runs	Wkts	Avg	RPO	BB	5I	10M
Boland	13	23	1	1056	202 *	48.00	3	4	15	0	1099	355	24	14.79	1.93	4-25	0	0
Derbyshire	60	98	8	2813	217	31.25	3	16	81	0	2688	2108	98	21.51	2.69	5-63	1	0
Eastern Province	8	14	0	813	142	58.07	3	4	7	0	1092	525	19	27.63	2.88	3-21	0	0
Transvaal	30	53	7	1855	212	40.32	5	9	26	0	3617	1693	56	30.23	2.80	4-28	0	0
Transvaal B	6	10	0	227	72	22.70	0	1	9	0	0	0	0	-	-	-	0	0
Western Province	82	146	6	5024	163	35.88	12	21	111	0	12812	5132	243	21.11	2.40	7-24	11	1

First-class matches by competition

Competition	M	Inns	NO	Runs	HS	Avg	100	50	Ct	St	Balls	Runs	Wkts	Avg	RPO	BB	5I	10M
Currie Cup "A Section"	97	178	10	6413	212	38.17	16	30	117	0	14967	6234	264	23.61	2.49	7-24	7	1
Currie Cup "B Section"	25	39	1	1468	202 *	38.63	4	5	35	0	2004	647	53	12.20	1.93	7-26	3	0
All Currie Cup	122	217	11	7881	212	38.25	20	35	152	0	6971	6881	317	21.70	2.43	7-24	10	1
County Championship	56	92	7	2685	217	31.58	3	14	77	0	4346	1915	89	21.51	2.64	5-63	1	0

All List A limited overs matches

M	Inns	NO	Runs	HS	Avg	100	50	Ct	St	Balls	Runs	Wkts	Avg	RPO	BB	4I
100	99	4	3013	186	31.71	3	22	43	0	5058	2950	162	18.20	3.49	6-33	4

TEST RECORD

Date	Test	Venue	Opp.	1st Inns	2nd Inns	Batting	Ct	Result
08/12/61	1	Durban	NZ	8-3-17-0	dnb	15 & 10	1	Won
26/12/61	2	Johannesburg	NZ	3-0-15-0	3-2-5-0	47 & 45	1	Draw
01/01/62	3	Cape Town	NZ	9-0-40-0	20-2-53-0	51 & 16	2	Lost
02/02/62	4	Johannesburg	NZ	dnb	dnb	67 & dnb	0	Won
16/02/62	5	Port Elizabeth	NZ	dnb	dnb	20 & 59	1	Lost
06/12/63	1	Brisbane	Aus	9-0-71-1	dnb	114 & 0	2	Draw
01/01/64	2	Melbourne	Aus	7.6-0-51-2	11-0-49-1	109 & 54	0	Lost
10/01/64	3	Sydney	Aus	2-0-9-0	1-0-5-0	6 & 35	1	Draw
24/01/64	4	Adelaide	Aus	dnb	5-2-6-3	201 & 47*	0	Won
07/02/64	5	Sydney	Aus	9-1-31-0	1-0-8-0	5 & 32*	2	Draw
21/02/64	1	Wellington	NZ	11-0-38-0	2-1-13-0	22 & 92	1	Draw
28/02/64	2	Dunedin	NZ	3-0-11-0	dnb	49 & 13	0	Draw
13/03/64	3	Auckland	NZ	12-5-20-2	16-8-19-0	61 & 58	1	Draw
04/12/64	1	Durban	Eng	20-5-36-0	dnb	2 & 0	0	Lost
23/12/64	2	Johannesburg	Eng	8-2-33-0	dnb	71 & 15	0	Draw
01/01/65	3	Cape Town	Eng	12-3-37-1	dnb	138 & 78	2	Draw
22/01/65	4	Johannesburg	Eng	18-5-34-1	dnb	96 & 42	4	Draw
12/02/65	5	Port Elizabeth	Eng	22-2-55-3	dnb	69 & 47	1	Draw
22/07/65	1	Lord's	Eng	19-6-31-0	9-1-25-0	1 & 52	2	Draw
05/08/65	2	Nottingham	Eng	dnb	7-1-20-0	19 & 76	0	Won

Date	Test	Venue	Opp.	1st Inns	2nd Inns	Batting	Ct	Result
26/08/65	3	The Oval	Eng	11-1-27-0	6-1-22-0	18 & 18	1	Draw
23/12/66	1	Johannesburg	Aus	17-3-39-3	15-1-47-1	13 & 50	0	Won
31/12/66	2	Cape Town	Aus	33.3-9-85-5	2-1-1-0	19 & 17	0	Lost
20/01/67	3	Durban	Aus	11-4-18-3	14-5-28-0	0 & 22	2	Won
03/02/67	4	Johannesburg	Aus	11-6-25-1	7-3-20-0	4 & dnb	0	Draw
24/02/67	5	Port Elizabeth	Aus	4-2-9-0	15-3-52-2	46 & 15	1	Won
22/01/70	1	Cape Town	Aus	1-0-15-0	6-2-14-0	127 & 16	4	Won
05/02/70	2	Durban	Aus	10-3-24-3	31-10-63-3	1 & dnb	1	Won
19/02/70	3	Johannesburg	Aus	12-5-31-0	7-3-17-2	6 & 110	0	Won
05/03/70	4	Port Elizabeth	Aus	9-1-27-1	18-3-66-2	73 & 27	3	Won

Summary of all matches

M	Runs	HS	Ave	100s	50s	W	BB	Ave	5w	Ct
30	2516	201	45.75	6	15	40	5-85	34.05	1	33

Appendix C

A Derbyshire poem

This poem was written and read by James Graham Brown as a tribute to Eddie Barlow, at the end of his three seasons as captain of Derbyshire County Cricket Club.

There was once a Derbyshire Sec
Who saw that his club was a wreck
So to hold the ship steady
He sent for King Eddie
Then went to the bank for the cheque.

Now things weren't that great with the Derbyshire state
But they weren't as bad as all that
But they did have a bowler and a new heavy roller
And a couple of guys who could bat.

But the pride of the side could not be denied
He was the illustrious snatcher
Who at the sight of a chance would make a small dance
And dive in the air and catch 'er.

When the new King arrived to take over the side
He looked at the faces, all new
Some tall, some short, good heavens, he thought
What a motley crew.

In the corner, he saw what he'd not seen before
A nude man who was holding a bat
Who twitched in his stance like St Vitus's dance
And moved like a scalded cat.

In the opposite seat sat a fellow, quite neat
But whose hair was just like a Brillo
He was saying, "If you flick it, it will go through mid-wicket
Despite the weight of your willow".

And in the middle with many a riddle
Sat the joker of the pack
He was a charmer, this jovial left-armer
Who had just come back from the sack.

His stories were old and oft had been told
But still they served to console us
They were tales of woe, of life and so,
But most of Brian Bolus.

Well, King Eddie was quiet as he watched the riot
Of players all arguing madly
And he knew if he tried to make them a side
They wouldn't do quite so badly.

So the good King rose and everyone froze
At the sight of his massive frame
Even the gang Dickie Pogie stopped in their roguery
And bowed their heads in shame.

If you've not heard of this gang
They're the men who rang the phones to each hotel room
And changed the papers and did other capers
Before they met their doom.

So up stood King Eddie
And held himself steady
And delivered a powerful speech
He spoke of cricket, of runs and wickets
And of the new goals to reach.

So along with Duke Russell
He built sinew and muscle
In each of the Derbyshire team
And the lads ran in style, the four-minute mile
And did press-ups by the ream.

So the bowlers bowled longer
And the strokes got stronger
And the fielders ran all day
Thus growing more able they crept up the table
And only moaned for more pay.

So, you'll leave us next season
With a team that with reason
Should go to work like a charm
And back in Cape Town, you'll be wearing a frown
As you clean out the sties on your farm.

So thank you Ed for the way that you've led
This wonderful Derbyshire side
For an epitaph from your playing staff
"C'MON, WATCH," he cried.

Postscript
by Cally Barlow

At 11.58am on December 30th, 2005 at the Jersey General Hospital, with my daughter Fiona holding his right hand and me holding his left hand, my darling Eds exhaled his last breath.

Christmas had been wonderful, with Fiona and her family in Jersey. We all had great presents, the table looked a picture, the food was outstanding and the grandsons had practised Away in a Manger, which they sang after lunch. We were quiet on Boxing Day and the day after.

On the afternoon of December 28th, Fiona and I decided to walk down to town and do a little shopping. Mike would pick us up later after he had taken Eddie and my Mother out for a drive. Fiona's mobile phone rang and it was Henry. He told us to come back quickly as Eddie had had a fall and they could not stop the bleeding from his nose.

We leaped into a taxi and arrived back to see Eds sitting in a chair with blood everywhere. I asked Mike what had happened and he said he had left Eddie at the front door to go and open the car door and when he turned round Eds was on the ground. We called the ambulance, as it was very evident that I was not going to be able to stop the bleeding. He seemed fine on the way to the hospital and he was taken in to the emergency unit.

While we were in the waiting room, we heard the doctor say "Eddie stay with us, stay with us". Fiona and I looked at each other in horror. What on earth had happened?

Eventually, the doctor came to us and said that Eddie had suffered a brain haemorrhage. They had sent the X-rays to Southampton but the doctors there had said it was not possible to operate because the haemorrhage had been too severe. He was in a coma and even if he came out of it, they said he would have no meaningful life. I tried to explain what the doctors had said before when he had the first stroke, but they assured me that this was different. I was in total shock, then turmoil.

What on earth should I do? I did remember Eddie telling me that he would not want to live if he could not move. He had been upset enough about not having the use of his left hand but this was something else. How could I make the decision to turn off the ventilator? In the end, I rang Helen, his first wife, to ask her what to do. She agreed with me that Eds would have hated being completely incapacitated and that the right thing to do was turn it off.

That evening I went into the hospital with Fiona and her boys, Henry, Ruaridh and Hamish, to see Eddie and for the grandchildren to say their goodbyes. I told them that Eddie was not very pretty because of the fall but they still wanted to go in to see him. One by one, we went in and they talked to him and gave him a kiss goodbye. We sat in the waiting room with them afterwards and Ruaridh and Hamish wanted to go in again. Ruaridh had brought one of his tickly things, a piece of orange gauzy material that he had used since being a tiny one when he was drinking his milk. "I want this to be roasted with Eddie," he said, and so we tied it round his wrist.

I had brought in a CD of Katherine Jenkins which Eddie adored and the nurse let me play it for him as we were the only ones in intensive care at the time. She was brilliant and when I asked if I could stay the night she said of course, and she then did something so wonderful I will never ever forget it.

She got one of the other beds and pushed it right next to Eddie's and then used the huge sheets and blankets to cover both of us, so that I was able to hold my darling Eddie for just one more night, to tell him how much I loved him and that he would always be in my heart.

The following morning Fiona came back and, at just after 10.00 am, the nurse removed the ventilator and we sat on either side of him holding his hands. We talked to him and told stories and Katherine Jenkins played in the background.

I was watching his face and listening to him breathing and at 11.58 am he drew a big breath, let it slowly out and died.

When we got back to Fiona's house the boys were there and we were trying to put a brave face on things when Ruaridh said "Mama, where has Eddie gone?"

How to explain to an eight-year-old? Wanting Eds to remain a part of us all I said: "Ruaridh, we cannot see him but he is sitting on my shoulder looking after me now."

Hamish came up to me and said "Hello Eds", and stroked my shoulder. It was the beginning of something wonderful.

On their first day back at school, Fiona was called in by Ruaridh's teacher because he had been so upset. The next day I walked down with him and he said to me, "You know, Mama, I am going to be really upset when you leave me".

I thought quickly and said to him. "I'll tell you what, Ruaridh, I will take Eddie off my shoulder and put him on your shoulder and he will look after you for today."

We had a solemn passing-over ceremony and when I went to pick him up later I asked him how it had gone.

"Great, Mama," he replied. "I took Eddie to football and he helped me to score three goals."

Eddie's daughter and son, Susan and Craig, both came over to Jersey for the cremation and it was such a support for me. The flowers on the coffin were yellow roses with bright shiny green leaves, the green and gold of South Africa, and the grandchildren had put their last messages in with them. We had all his favourites at the service – 'I vow to thee my country', 'Abide with Me', 'Do not stand at my grave and weep', 'Trevor Huddleston's poem', 'Violet Szabo's last message to her daughter, which I altered slightly to make it more fitting, and part of the poem by EV Thompson about my Barlow long ago. At the end of the service, he had the Celtic Blessing.

Afterwards we toasted Eds as he would have wished, with plenty of red wine at a magnificent wake put on by Malcolm Lewis, owner of Longueville Manor, the very best hotel on the island.

I was not particularly looking forward to going out to South Africa for the two memorial services, first at Pretoria Boys High School and then at St Saviour's and Newlands in Cape Town, but they both turned out to be wonderful occasions.

Verity Ross looked after me wonderfully well in Johannesburg, while

Peter Cooke and Don MacRobert kindly looked after all the arrangements for the service in Pretoria. Bossie Clarke and Andre Odendaal admirably took care of everything in Cape Town. At one stage, Peter and Don asked what I wanted to be inscribed, not only on a plaque they were putting in the Memorial wall at PBHS, but also on a bench beside the cricket field.

I came up with:

> *Bold in outlook*
> *Unfailingly honest*
> *Never afraid*
>
> *Totally committed*
> *Ever a friend*
> *Rest peacefully*

People cope with death in many different ways and each one is right for the person involved. I feel totally overcome by his going as he was my strength just as much as I was his. I cope with his death by really feeling that his spirit is with me and, above all, by talking about him, watching videos to hear his lovely voice, looking at all the photographs I have, reading the cuttings and keeping his memory alive. My grandsons and I still have "Ed power".

I only knew Eddie for a relatively short time but I loved him above everything. For me, and many others, his act will never be followed.